POLITICS AND SUSTAINABLE GROWTH IN THE ARCTIC

Politics and Sustainable Growth in the Arctic

Edited by Jyrki Käkönen
Tampere Peace Research Institute

Dartmouth
Aldershot • Brookfied USA • Hong Kong • Singapore • Sydney

© Jyrki Käkönen 1993

All rights reserved. No part of this publication may be reproduced, stored in a retrieval system, or transmitted in any form or by any means, electronic, mechanical, photocopying, recording, or otherwise without the prior permission of Dartmouth Publishing Company Limited.

Published by
Dartmouth Publishing Company Limited
Gower House
Groft Road
Aldershot
Hants GU11 3HR
England

Dartmouth Publishing Company
Old Post Road
Brookfield
Vermont 05036
USA

HC
733
.P65
1993

A CIP catalogue record for this book is available from the British Library

ISBN 1 85521 333 8

Printed and Bound in Great Britain by
Athenaeum Press Ltd, Newcastle upon Tyne

Contents

Tables and figures — vii

Preface — ix

Contributors — xi

1 Introduction
  Jyrki Käkönen — 1

2 Peripheries in a changing world order
  W.L. Goldfrank — 5

3 Growth-oriented economy, development and sustainable development
  Jyrki Käkönen — 15

4 Arctic development, environment and northern natives in Russia
  Alexei Yu. Roginko — 25

5 Arctic haze: an exploration of international regime alternatives
  Marvin S. Soroos — 35

6 Sustainable security: an Inuit perspective
  Dalee Sambo — 51

v

7	The role of Sami traditions in sustainable development *Elina Helander*	67
8	Knowledge-based development in the North: new approaches to sustainable development *J.D. House*	81
9	Financial resources for sustainable development in the Arctic *Michael Pretes*	93

Index 107

Tables and figures

Table 3.1 Four fold of security and development   22

Table 5.1 International Regime Alternatives for Addressing
          Arctic Haze   41

Figure 7.1 General map of the Sami areas in Norway, Finland,
           Sweden and Russia   68

Figure 9.1 The Relationship Between Metropolis and Satellite.
           Adapted from Frank (1969)   95

Table 9.1 Characteristics of Present, Transition Stage, and
          Future Peripheral Economies   99

Figure 9.2 The Relationship Between Permanent Trust Fund
           Income (1) and Non-Renewable Resource Income (2)   101

Figure 9.3 A Sample Trust Fund Structure. The Structure Shown is
           that of the Alaska Permanent Fund   103

Preface

The Tampere Peace Research Institute launched an Arctic Research project in 1987, originally as part of the TAPRI Workshops on 'European Futures; Bases and Choices'. The workshops were financed in large part by a generous grant from the John D. and Catherine T. MacArthur Foundation. During 1988-1990, under the workshop programme, the project's title was 'Alternative Development and Security in the Arctic'; now, in 1991-1993, we are working under a new title: 'Sustainable Development and Security in the Arctic'.

The project has been very much an international effort. We have had a number of international seminars and discussed the contributions of many scholars. This publication is largely based on papers that were first presented at a seminar that was held in Inari, Finland in May 1991. The papers have been revised, and some additional contributions have been solicited.

I would like to take this opportunity to thank all the contributors as well as all the participants at the seminar who helped to inspire a lively debate and who in that capacity contributed to the work of the project.

Jyrki *Käkönen*
17 June 1992
Fuengirola, Spain

Contributors

Walter *Goldfrank*, professor of sociology, California State University, Santa Cruz.

Elina *Helander*, director, Nordic Sami Institute, Kautokeino, Norway.

Douglas *House*, doctor, Economic Recovery Commission, Newfoundland and Labrador, St. John's.

Jyrki *Käkönen*, director, Tampere Peace Research Institute, Tampere, Finland.

Michael *Pretes*, research fellow, Research Institute for Northern Finland, Rovaniemi.

Alexei *Roginko*, senior research fellow, Institute for World Economy and International Relations (IMEMO), Moscow.

Dalee *Sambo*, executive director, International Union for Circumpolar Health, Anchorage, Alaska.

Marvin *Soroos*, professor of political science, North Carolina State University, Raleigh.

1 Introduction

Jyrki Käkönen

The articles in this volume have been written for the research project on 'Sustainable Development and Security in the Arctic', which was launched by the Tampere Peace Research Institute (TAPRI) during the latter half of the 1980s when the Cold War was drawing to an end. At that time there was one single issue that commanded most of the attention of researchers: the militarization of the Arctic. Now, following the collapse of the Soviet Union, the strategic role of the Arctic has changed. The military hardware is still there, but it is a much lesser threat than it was during the years of bipolarism.

From a military point of view the future strategic role of the Arctic will depend very much on the foreign and defence policies of Russia. Those policies, it should be clear by now, will be different from those pursued by the Soviet Union. In the meantime, while Russia is hammering out its new policies, there should be sufficient incentive to develop a new international policy and to integrate Russia into an Arctic peace order.

With the old antagonisms behind us, there is indeed an excellent opportunity now to bring in a new policy of cooperation in the Arctic, a policy that would have important benefits for the whole population living in the region. One might also argue that the declining strategic significance of the Arctic presents a good opportunity to raise other issues that are vital for the future existence of the region. In fact, the time is now right for creating a strategy for sustainable development in the Arctic.

Sustainable development and security have been among the main topics of TAPRI's Arctic project from the very outset. The changes we have seen in the international system have not changed our priorities. On the contrary, the declining military significance of the Arctic gives added weight to other, civilian issues. In this sense the present collection of articles by the scholars who cooperated with us in TAPRI's Arctic project has perhaps even greater value than we thought when we started planning this report.

However, the changing international environment has given cause not only to optimism but also to a sense of pessimism. At the outset our assumption was that the Arctic needs an alternative development and security policy. We also thought that a regional strategy for sustainable development in the Arctic was possible. This assumption was based on at least two things: First, the Arctic was and still is one of the least polluted areas in the world, although at the same time nature in the Arctic is extremely vulnerable. Second, the Arctic was only marginally industrialized and modernized in spite of its huge natural resources. So perhaps it would not be necessary to repeat all the mistakes that had been made elsewhere during the process of industrialization and modernization.

There have been many disappointments. The project has taught us that the Arctic is not an isolated region; it has long since been integrated into the national systems of the northernmost states as well as into the whole international system. This means that the role of the Arctic is restricted to that of a periphery, a role prescribed by the centre. We have, consequently, had to change our perspective. In this report our intention is to find out what sort of alternatives are available to an integrated peripheral region in a unifying international system.

In the first article professor Walter Goldfrank looks at the role of peripheries in the world system context, a context in which the future of the peripheries does not seem very promising. They have always been and apparently always will be remote resource-providing areas for the centres. The Arctic is one of the last frontiers, and it too will be turned into to a resource-producing region. In the second article, I myself present the assumption that in the current world system there is no room for a sustainable development in the Arctic. Any attempt at a sustainable development in the periphery presupposes a change in the centre. This means that the responsibility for the future development of the whole globe as well as of local regions lies with the centres of the world system.

The article by doctor Alexei Roginko gives a detailed account of how the Soviet Arctic was integrated into the Soviet system. This remote region was one of the very foundations of the development of Soviet society. However, as a resource area it was used for the benefit of the centre. The small Arctic nations were underdeveloped, and they had to pay the costs. Even today, the future of these nations in Russia remains open. However, as Russia is even more dependent on its Arctic resources than the Soviet Union ever was, it is difficult to see how there could be any major changes. Finally, one may also ask whether the destiny of the small Russian Arctic nations is going to be repeated in other parts of the Arctic.

This pessimistic vision is partly supported by professor Marvin Soroos's interesting article on the Arctic haze. The Arctic haze is a result of the industrialization and modernization of the centres, which means that even in the field of air pollution the Arctic is deeply integrated into the international system. This, in turn, means that regional solutions for environmental protection are rarely sufficient. An international environmental regime is required to save the Arctic environment. On the other hand, regimes only regulate the pollution rather than tackle and solve the problem. The Arctic case also demonstrates the point that a scarce population tends to slow down efforts to solve environmental problems. This brings us back to the vital role of the centres.

These pessimistic visions are counterbalanced in this report by viewpoints on the way of life and values of the Arctic indigenous peoples. However, this perspective has no chance without the permission of the centre. In her article Dalee Sambo shows how integration has caused destruction, insofar as it is possible to talk about the dialectics of destruction and modernization. Modernization is threatening the natural order of things in Alaska as well as in the whole Arctic. On the other hand, the traditional way of life has much to offer to sustainable development. However, in the process of modernization cultural codes of adapting social life into the frames of the Arctic nature are disappearing. This is a process comparable to the disappearance of the genetic heritage of the globe.

Director Elina Helander stresses the same aspects. The traditional knowledge of the Sami people, she says, can contribute fruitfully to our understanding of sustainable development. In Northern Europe, as well as in the whole Arctic region, the process of modernization is threatening this traditional knowledge as well as the ecological traditions of the native people. Sambo and Helander both point out that ecological degradation also represents a serious threat to traditional indigenous cultures. This same argument also appears in the article by Roginko. In order to control their own destiny, indigenous peoples need to enjoy full autonomy; this is the precondition for sustainable development. But once again, autonomy requires the permission of the centres of power.

Another perspective for an optimistic alternative is provided by modernization. Doctor Douglas House argues for a sustainable development which is based on decentralized systems. His example is the development policy of Labrador and Newfoundland, where development has been largely based on knowledge. This kind of changing role for the periphery in the world system requires new and adaptive technology. In this kind of alternative setting the economy cannot be based on the utilization of exhausting resources but on adaptive knowledge.

In the last article of the book Michael Pretes outlines an alternative basis for decentralized and locally administrated economic activities. According to his vision the utilization of non-renewable resources and Arctic megaprojects should finance trust funds for sustainable Arctic development, which would accumulate resources for local development and, more importantly, provide resources from exhausting reserves for future generations. But once again, the critical point is that these funds cannot operate without the blessing of the centres. In a global perspective, this means that a small minority in the centres of the world system is responsible for the options of sustainable development as well as for the options of future generations.

2 Peripheries in a changing world order

W. L. Goldfrank

On December 12, (1990) charges of arson, mischief, possession of explosives and disguise with intent were laid against 13 people of the Lubicon (Cree) Nation in Northern Alberta. They are accused of sabotaging the logging equipment of Buchanan Lumber, which has recently begun logging in unceded Lubicon lands despite assurances that all development not authorized by them, the rightful owners of the territory, would be dismantled. They called this "direct action on the ground." The Lubicon struggle is one for survival. Already, moose, the traditional dietary staple, has "disappeared" from their land. One in every three Lubicon now has tuberculosis, compared to 1 in every 15,000 Canadians. Unemployment is at 95% and the community is forced into dependency on welfare. All this while oil and gas revenues reaped by Canadian and multinational corporations (Petro-Can, for instance) total over $1 million a day. The Lubicon hold to their sovereignty in responding to the charges; they claim that the province of Alberta has no jurisdiction on sovereign Lubicon land and therefore that Nation members are not subject to Canadian Courts.

This story arrived in my computer by electronic mail, one day during the bombardment of Iraq. It is a story told many times before, and, in different versions, one that will be told many times again. It is a story of intensified exploitation of the peripheral zones of the modern world-system, of incorporating land (and the land's resources) and/or labor (when necessary to production). It is never a pretty story, and it is one that those who benefit directly or indirectly prefer not to hear, much less to tell, unless they recast it in terms of heroic military adventure against the savages, devoted religious conversion of the heathens, or intrepid entrepreneurship to bring new comforts or pleasures to the civilized. In the currently unfashionable language of Karl Marx, it is a story of primitive (or primary) accumulation.

Marx, however, merely thought that the plunder of alien culture and nature, and the expropriation of subsistence peoples, were necessary to start the whole capitalist accumulation process, providing, as it were, the "M" (money-capital), and the labor-power component of the "C" (commodities) for the ceaseless equation M+C=M. However, in the understanding of the world-system perspective which is my own, the processes of primitive accumulation continue long after purely "capitalist" accumulation has been launched. Not only do they continue, albeit unevenly, but they are necessary to the reproduction and expansion of the capitalist system as we know it in the world today.

In what follows, my aims will be first, to sketch an overview of our understanding of how the modern world works; second, to specify some different types of peripheral zones; and third, to adumbrate some possible futures for the peripheries. In brief, I shall make two substantive assertions: 1) that in its proximate long cycles world capitalism will transform the remaining peripheral reserve lands into resource-yielding territories and will transform the remaining subsistence foragers, pastoralists, and peasants into proletarians; and 2) that peripheral zones within core states will fare significantly better than those in semi-peripheral and peripheral states, albeit at great cultural and environmental cost. Allow me to begin, then, by showing you the lens through which I see the world.

The modern world-system is a capitalist world-economy encompassing virtually the entire globe, although as a system its 16th-century original scope was limited territorially to parts of Europe and the Americas. Historically changing, it is nonetheless a system, a structured totality whose parts both complement and affect one another. We call it a world-economy because its commodity chains link disparate peoples and cultures via the market, unlike a world-empire, which links peoples by way of a politico-administrative apparatus. We call it capitalist because accumulation is its driving force, because labor is thereby commodified, and because competition and class struggle are its hallmarks, competition and struggle that occur across as well as within state boundaries. We understand this division into classes to intersect a division into zones, some with great wealth, sophisticated and diversified production, and strong states (the core), some with little wealth, low-wage production, and weak states (the periphery), and some in between on these dimensions (the semi-periphery). By means of plunder, labor migration, capital flight, and unequal exchange, surplus moves from the periphery to the core, as it does in the production process from labor to capital. Over historical time the locus of particular products shifts from one to another zone, as for example iron and steel production has in the last decades been moving from the core to the semi-periphery. And there is limited mobility for states as the system as a whole has expanded, mobility we can see in the recent rise of Taiwan and South Korea from periphery to semi-periphery or the ascents of Italy and Finland from semi-periphery to core since World War II. But the massive fact about the modern world-system to date is its reproduced stability, as capitalist commodification has penetrated more and more of the globe and proletarianized more and more of its inhabitants, and as the interstate mix of diplomacy and war has contained and reprogrammed rebellious oppositional movements.

Further, we understand this modern world-system to move through time both cyclically and via secular trends. The cycles are economic and political: economically, the world undergoes 50-60 year long waves of expansion and stagnation (sometimes called A and B phases), increasingly yet still imperfectly synchronized in their various national manifestations. Politically, the world experiences much longer cycles of hegemony, with four phases, which we may call ascent through conflict, supremacy, decline, and condominium. The secular trends at work are familiar to students of modernity: commodification (including labor), mechanization of production, bureaucratization of organizations, and last, geographical expansion, the process of incorporating previously external areas into the system, with very rare exceptions as peripheries. But we understand these trends to be constitutive of rather than external to the world-system, and we understand their limits, which we shall reach within a century or two, to presage a crisis from which a new politico-economic form of global social organization will emerge.

Given this perspective, the contemporary world appears as follows. Leaving aside some of the controversial and/or borderline cases, the core of the world economy includes the USA and Canada, most of Western and Northern Europe, and Japan. Core countries are relatively wealthy and relatively democratic, specializing in high-technology products such as computers, aerospace, and machine tools, producing abundant food, experiencing shrinkage in industrial employment and growth in the so-called service sector (much of which is of course part of the production process). The contemporary semi-periphery includes most of Eastern Europe and Russia, at least the more industrial countries of Latin America, South Africa, Turkey, and the East Asian NICs. These countries feature heavy intermediate industrial production (iron and steel, petrochemicals), strong but diminishing state control of the economy, enormous debt burdens, and much of the democratization wave of the last decade. Their working classes are increasing in social power (Arrighi 1990), but this makes for increasing difficulty in resolving economic policy dilemmas, especially where statist protectionism of the socialist or populist variety have been prevalent.

The contemporary periphery includes the poorer countries of Latin America and the Caribbean, most of sub-Saharan Africa, South and Southeast Asia, and China. Most of the world's two billion peasants live in the periphery; with their compatriots who are no longer peasants they produce an array of raw materials and simple manufactures (textiles, assembly). They live for the most part under authoritarian regimes and face the stark alternatives of exclusion from the world economy (as rulers in Myanmar and Kampuchea chose for a time) or superexploitation within it. Note as well three complications of this very broad-brush sketch. The peripheral giants China, India, and to a degree Pakistan and Indonesia as well include substantial heavy industrial sectors similar to those in the semi-periphery.

At the same time, many of the larger semi-peripheral countries contain significant peripheral areas within their national boundaries, such as the Brazilian Northeast and Amazonia, the Mexican South, some of the USSR (Central Asia, the far North), Kurdistan, and the South African Bantustans. There remain some peripheral pockets within the boundaries of the core states themselves, parts of Appalachia and the Southwestern desert in the USA, perhaps parts of Extremadura and Andalusia in Spain, the interior of Corsica (France), Sardinia, and Sicily (Italy), and the Arctic zones of Scandinavia, Canada, and the USA (Alaska).

In terms of the cycles and trends outlined earlier, where do we stand today? Politically, we are experiencing the end of US hegemony and its transmutation into trilateral condominium. The political manoeuvring that surrounded the Gulf massacre showed a confusing mix of old-style US unilateralism plus hat-in-hand begging and UN resolutions and authorizations. The State Department inclined toward the new multilateralism, the Defence Department toward the old unilateralism. The President wavered, one foot in each era. In the end, the old predominated, but with a heavy ideological emphasis on the coalition, the alliance, the UN. So if for the moment the US has a near-monopoly on usable tactical military might, this seems less the expression of a robust hegemony than a specialized function within a condominium of core powers, the emergency police of the world-system.

Economically, the world is approaching the end of a long wave that included the great post-war boom of the 1950s and 60s, and the slowdown of the 1970s and 80s. As with previous booms, a rising tide floated many boats, yielding some now rather quaint beliefs: that the core countries had solved the problem of crises by fiscal and monetary fine tuning, that the self-styled socialist countries would catch up (remember Khrushchev's "we will bury you" or the once-fashionable idea of "convergence" between the USA and the USSR?), that the periphery should be called "developing" nations in "the springtime of freedom." The downturn of the 1970s and 80s has been quite another story, however. Too much emphasis has been given to the exceptional successes during this B-phase, for example, to Japan and the East Asian NICs, which greatly resemble the advances in Germany and some of its eastern neighbors during the depressed last quarter of the nineteenth century. What requires a longer look are the declines, the disasters, the catastrophes, in most of the periphery and much of the semi-periphery as well, as the gap between the haves and have-nots of the world has grown larger.

The catastrophic losses of lives and livelihoods to floods, droughts, and earthquakes speak volumes about the injustices and irrationalities of a world that wastes billions of dollars on armaments. It is not for me to say how much is nature's toll and how much society's; having survived both devastating floods and a major earthquake in my own microregion of California, I am inclined to absolve nature. Inadequate infrastructure, impoverished health and nutrition systems, insubstantial emergency organization, these are the major culprits. But catastrophe is just the tip of an iceberg. As Ghai and Hewitt de Alcantara show, Africa, Latin America, and the Caribbean have undergone crises "of unprecedented proportions" (1989, p. 1). In Africa real GDP per capita fell 25% between 1980 and 1988, per capita income 30%; for Latin America and the Caribbean, the comparable declines are 7% and 15%. They focus on four principal causal factors: deteriorating terms of trade, high interest rates, declines in credits and investments, and capital flight. They point out that the negative effects of the crisis have hit poorer countries harder than more prosperous ones, middle and working classes harder than the wealthy. They cite evidence even of "repeasantization" in Ghana and in Mexico.

Writing of Latin America, Cornia and Jesperson (1989) show the distressing effects of the crisis on the health and nutrition of children, via higher food prices and declining incomes, lower government food subsidies and health expenditures, and child neglect as women in desperation enter the informal sector labor market. Focusing on the Caribbean, Thomas (1989, p. 8) discusses a similar array of problems but paints an even grimmer picture by discussing technical and economic changes that will tend to increase the gap between the peripheral zones and the core. "Technical changes in the areas of robotics, information, and transport are leading to losses in the region's wage cost-location-propinquity advantages in relation to the US-Canadian market" (Thomas 1989, p. 8). He adds that advances in materials science are devaluing the region's raw materials (especially true for sugar and bauxite-alumina), that flexible specialization in the clothing industry and migration to New York are hurting the islands' needle trades, and that new systems of information management are threatening the offshore financial sector. To summarize, the recent past has been disastrous for many peripheral zones, nor are the immediate prospects very promising.

Let us consider more carefully some differences among peripheries. What are the major axes for typologizing? Most important are structural location within the world-system, resource and/or geo-strategic potentialities, population density, and, ethno-cultural distinctiveness. Low-density descendants of European settlers who live in resource-laden lands within core states are at one extreme in their chances for general well-being; high-density indigenes occupying barren lands in peripheral states are at the other extreme. Compare here Appalachia in the USA with East Bengal before the break-up of Pakistan. Because of opportunities to migrate to Cincinnati, Chicago, and other cities, because of structural access to strong representation by federal legislators, and because of locational and political (non-union) attractiveness to multinational industrial investors, the Appalachians have improved their situation over the last several decades to the point at which it makes little sense to characterize them as peripheral, if it ever did, though consciousness of being an "internal colony" has been part of the intellectual atmosphere there for some time (see Newman 1972 for an appraisal of regional development programs in the 1960s, and Batteau 1983 for a review of newer "dependencies"). The Bengalis of East Pakistan had neither opportunity nor democratic access; by all indices of well-being they were among the poorest people in the world thank God for fish. Their political independence has scarcely brought improvements, but then the economic conjuncture has been worse since independence than before, and substitutes for jute in the global fibre industry have further increased their resource poverty. It has required a major catastrophe to call world attention to their plight, and they stand to receive charitable contributions that will do more to assuage the consciences of the well-off than to address the structural inequalities that perpetuate their misery.

To these extreme types we should add another: Antarctica, a vast continent whose riches have barely begun to be exploited. Thus far, krill harvests, primarily by the Soviet fleet, are the only extractive activity. Since Antarctica is uninhabited, its exploitation is subject merely to environmental constraints and to those arising from interstate conflicts. In a fascinating article, Rosh (1989, p. 129) has shown that the marine, petroleum, mineral, and fresh water resources of the southernmost continent are scarcely regulated by the current treaty, which establishes "an exclusive real estate club that is not recognized as legitimate by most of the world's states". Some states assert exclusive rights over resources in the sectors they have claimed, while others the most technologically advanced want nondiscriminatory access. Claims of some semi-peripheral and large peripheral states have divided the Third World, and weakened its efforts to make Antarctica part of the Common Heritage of Humankind.

If we move from the extreme types toward the center, we find an array of zones and peoples whose ways of life are also defined by their relationship to core projects. From the point of view of cultural continuity, it is probably advantageous to inhabit economically marginal and strategically negligible land. Certain mountain- and desert-dwellers fit this description, but there is always the threat that mineral deposits will be discovered or rendered accessible by advances in mining or transportation technology. Such groups live at the sufferance of the powerful, but in core countries, if less so in the semi-periphery, they present little threat and elicit considerable sympathy from the liberal middle class. Forest and jungle dwellers are under even more pressure; exploitation of their traditional lands poses dangers not only to them but to the globe, via rising core levels.

From the somewhat contradictory standpoint of improved living standards and/or security of livelihood, however, it is probably advantageous to reside in a resource-rich or strategically crucial territory. In this instance, the economic possibilities range from a rentier relationship to the assets (via leasing arrangements or royalty payments), to part or full ownership, to the development of technical and managerial capacity to assure medium- to longrun profits for the community. A cursory review (Kruse et al. 1982, p. 97) of the effects of energy extraction among the Navajo in the US Southwest and Indians and Eskimo in Canada finds employment benefits accruing to a small elite of wage earners, collective royalty payments well below fair market value, and most expenditures made to off-reservation businesses. Unemployment continues at high levels and conventional social pathologies are found along with declining availability of fish and game in certain areas. On the other hand they cite one apparently successful case, among the Inuit, of rotating wage-labor providing cash for "family necessities and hunting equipment" (Kruse et al. 1982, p. 97) which increased the viability of customary subsistence practices.

Studies of resource extraction and food processing in Alaska furnish little basis for optimism in appraising the chances there for a happy marriage of indigenous cultural continuity and contemporary capitalist expansion. Current efforts are clearly preferable to the quasi-genocidal practices of settler colonization or coerced labor known in previous centuries. In their account of corporations founded under the Alaska Native Claims Settlement Act, Anders & Anders (1986, p. 232) suggest "limited prospects for achieving" economic and social goals given "conflicts between Native culture and ... profit-making functions." Encroachment on customary livelihood patterns has exacted a toll in suicide, homicide, alcoholism, and mental hospitalization rates far in excess of those for the European-descended population of the state. Anders & Anders note further the dangers of political backlash against a racial minority whom many feel "have been given too much already".

In their contrasting study of the Inupiat adaptation to North Slope oil extraction, Kruse et al. (1982) show how the creation of a local government "Borough" with access to tax revenues increased employment and cash income for many residents while enhancing the efficiency of many subsistence activities. Social problems were indeed serious, but the researchers found no increase in their severity owing to the introduction of petroleum extraction. Overall, the Inupiat are a sparse population in a vast territory; their revenues derive from a resource enclave in one corner of their lands, such that special circumstances may account for their relative success. But what will happen when the oil runs out? For Alaska as a whole, Ritter's (1979, p. 327) research suggests that as the native population has moved out of exclusively subsistence activities, "a quasi-cast-like cultural division of labor resulted", with natives in the bottom ranks of each occupational sector. This is likely to be the Inupiat fate as well.

Let us step back from our exploration of types of periphery and look toward the immediate and medium-term futures. As is characteristic of B phases in world-economic cycles, the present has witnessed an intensification of the secular trends characteristic of capitalist accumulation. Over the cries of environmentalists, geographic expansion into the last available territories is underway, in the Amazon and other tropical woodlands, in the Arctic and the Antarctic, even in the sea-bed; space exploitation remains at the level of science fiction. The social movements of indigenous peoples have gained a limited hearing at the UN and in liberal salons, but these Polanyi-esque movements to protect customary livelihoods have made little headway outside of the core countries; the assassination of Chico Mendes, leader of the Brazilian rubber-tappers might serve as a symbol here. New mechanization has been in process, preparing new product lines for widespread marketing when the world economy turns the corner toward accelerated growth at some point in the 90s. The most important of these processes appear to be microprocessing, genetic engineering, solar (and other renewable) energy, and robotics, and the peripheries will most probably be excluded from any profit opportunities in these sectors. But we should not rule out some benefits, e.g., from agricultural innovations, trickling down to the Third World. Democratization in much of the semi-periphery represents a potential for redistributing income such that the world market will expand, in turn sustaining new growth in the next A-phase. But the periphery is as conspicuous for its avoidance of democratization as the semi-periphery is for its tortured embrace.

In the short-run, after one or two further recessionary dips over the next few years, the accumulation process will accelerate as the world economy enters a new long wave. The leading high-technology sectors will return outsize profits to investors in Japan, Europe, and the US. Semi-peripheral competition for intermediate industrial production will intensify, and rebellious labor movements in democratized settings may well chase some of it to the periphery. Those semi-peripheral states with large peripheral zones will be sorely tempted to increase internal colonialism in order to keep pace or move forward, much as the Chilean state has recently fostered the overexploitation of forest and marine resources in the South, and the overexploitation of rural workers in the temperate central regions (Goldfrank 1989). Some peripheral exports may face replacement by novel materials, bringing further impoverishment, while others may turn out to be the 21st century's equivalent of petroleum in the 20th. But much of the periphery will be subjected to new forms of exploitation, much to disdainful exclusion punctuated by binges of charity. Meanwhile, the trend toward multinational corporate decomposition of production processes will gather momentum, making "national development" or national industrialization even more chimerical than they are today. In this scheme, labor-rich peripheries will continue to be invited to contribute low cost labor to certain stages in the production process, in the manner of scattered Export Processing Zones. But this will not have large multiplier effects.

If we shift our attention further into the future, to the middle-run 50-60 years of the new long wave, prediction becomes more difficult. Most probably, the currently visible trend toward forming three economic blocs around Japan, Europe, and the US will give way to a bipolar arrangement. A US/Japan alignment facing a European (West and East) agglomeration is more probable than any other. The Americas and the Pacific would be part of the former orbit, the Middle East probably part of the latter, with contestation between the blocs over India and sub-Saharan Africa. But this tendency toward bipolar bloc formation and rivalry will be dampened by a continuing trend toward a high degree of organizational integration among at least the core states at corporate, governmental, and associational levels (quite likely including labor). Because of growing international integration, hegemonic shifts, in the past occasions for world war, may in the future occur more peacefully, or perhaps not at all.

At the same time, significant new proletarianization in the semi-periphery and periphery will lead to the reinvigoration of oppositional movements, doubtless quite different from the Leninist model that prevailed for much of the 20th century. Heightened degradation of nature and increased exploitation of women will further stimulate such movements. For the first time in world history, not particular environments but the biosphere itself is threatened by human rapacity. Pressures for world state formation will come from core middle strata fearing disruption, nuclear proliferation, and environmental disaster. So too may they arise from semi-peripheral syndicalism after the OPEC model, and from Third World workers demanding global redistribution. In the absence of such redistribution, we are likely to see massive migratory movements toward the core, with increasing potential for ethnically or racially chauvinistic reaction.

Where, finally, do the peripheries within core states look to eventuate? First, there will be no stopping the extraction of valuable resources from these territories. Environmental and political constraints may bring to bear regulatory restrictions on these activities, but the momentum of capitalist expansion cannot be stopped over the medium run. Second, the relatively small size of the ethnic minority populations living in climates which their dominant fellow citizens find harsh and unappealing make it unlikely that they will be seen as a threat, so long as they do not interfere with resource extraction. Nor will these zones tend to attract significant migratory streams of non-indigenes. Third, increased access to cash income can enhance indigenous capabilities to continue customary subsistence practices, with perhaps some added danger of depleting nature. Fourth, the democratic structures and professed humane values of the core states render doubtful any reversal of the general post-war course toward a choice between supervised collective self-determination (resource use excepted) and individual assimilation. Pristine life-worlds have been irretrievably lost, cultural adaptation has exacted a heavy toll, but compared to the peripheries in the periphery, the middle-run future of the ultra-North offers promise as much as problems.

References

Anders, Gary C. and Anders, Kathleen K., 1986. 'Incompatible Goals in Unconventional Organizations: The Politics of Alaska Native Corporations', *Organization Studies*, Vol. 7. No. 3, pp. 213-33.

Arrighi, Giovanni, 1990. 'Marxist Century American Century: The Making and

Remaking of the World Labor Movement', pp. 54-95, in Samir Amin et al., *Transforming the Revolution*. New York: Monthly Review Press.

Batteau, Allen (ed.), 1983. *Appalachia and America: Autonomy and Regional Dependence*. Lexington, KY: The University Press of Kentucky.

Cornia, Giovanni A. and Jesperson, Eva, 1989. 'Crisis, Adjustment and Human Conditions: The Case of Latin America in the 1980s'. Paper presented at ISER (U. of West Indies) and UNRISD, Kingston, Jamaica, April 3-6.

Ghai, Dharam and Hewit de Alcantara, Cynthia, 1989. 'The Crisis of the 1980s in Africa, Latin America and the Caribbean: Economic Impact, Social Change and Political Implications'. Paper presented at ISER (U. of West Indies) and UNRISD, Kingston, Jamaica, April 3-6.

Goldfrank, Walter L., 1989. 'Harvesting Counter-revolution: Agricultural Exports in Pinochet's Chile', pp. 189-98, in Terry Boswell (ed.), *Revolution in the World-System*. Westport, CT: Greenwood Press.

Kruse, John A., Kleinfeld, Judith and Travis, Robert, 1982. 'Energy Development on Alaska's North Slope: Effects on the Inupiat Population', *Human Organization*, Vol. 41, No. 2, pp. 97-106.

Newman, Monroe, 1972. *The Political Economy of Appalachia*. Lexington, MA: D. C. Heath & Company.

Ritter, Kathleen V., 1979. 'Internal Colonialism and Industrial Development in Alaska', *Ethnic and Racial Studies*, Vol. 2, No. 3 (July), pp. 319-40.

Rosh, Robert M., 1989. 'Antarctica's Increasing Incorporation into the World-System', *Review*, Vol. XII, No. 1 (Winter), pp. 121-37.

Selden, Mark, 1988. 'City Versus Countryside? The social Consequences of Development Choices in China', *Review*, Vol. XI, No. 4 (Fall), pp. 533-68.

Thomas, Clive, 1989. 'The Economic Crisis and the Commonwealth Caribbean: Impact and Response'. Paper presented at ISER (U. of West Indies) and UNRISD, Kingston, Jamaica, April 3-6.

3 Growth-oriented economy, development and sustainable development

Jyrki Käkönen

1. Definitions

The conceptions mentioned in the title are problematic, because there exists no unanimity as to what they consist of. It is thus necessary to begin by explaining how and in what sense they are used in this article. One has to bear in mind, however, that exact definitions are hardly possible, maybe not even necessary. A loose definition renders it possible to handle the theme from varied angles.

In this context *growth-oriented economy* is understood as exploitation of nature by use of technology in order to produce such economic growth which enables the realization of the social policy aiming at economic and social equality (Adler-Karlsson 1990). *Development*, then, refers to the process of social change based on the conception of modernization in the development studies (see Hettne 1984). The process is creating greater and greater distance between society and nature (Connolly 1989). The change from agricultural society to urban industrial society is by definition seen as development. Similarly, the growing consumption produced by effective exploitation of nature is understood as a sign of development. *Sustainable development* is in this paper seen more or less similarly as in the Brundtland Commission's report, "Our Common Future" (1987). Development is there defined as sustainable as long as fulfilling the needs of this generation does not create limitations for the following generations and their chances to fulfil their needs.

Definitions like this naturally largely direct the course of examination. The definitions indicate that growth-oriented economy cannot be based on sustainable development. Production and consumption can be increased but natural resources are not cumulative. But the Brundtland Report (1987) states that sustainable development presupposes constant economic growth. In this view sustainable development is seen mainly as sustainable industrial development, and the basis of the social orientation and actions is not called into question.

At present there seem to be good reasons to be optimistic what comes to so called sustainable development and degradation of the environment. Most political parties in Europe have colored their programs greener: in their agenda environmental problems have got top priority. The decision makers of the mass consumption countries have also paid attention to the environmental issues. There is thus reason to believe that the overall environmental consciousness is both increasing and deepening. This should also lead to a clearer vision of nature as the basis of all human and social life.

A similar trend is perceivable in international politics. There already exists a growing pile of multilateral and bilateral international environmental agreements. All these phenomena can be understood as signs indicating that environmental problems can be managed in the context of growth-oriented economy. But is this interpretation a correct one? Or do we need to search for alternatives for the growth-oriented modernization project?

2. Environmental Problems as Crises of Growth-Oriented Development

Today's discussions of environmental politics concentrate clearly on the environmental heritage of socialism: the vast problems and even catastrophes.[1] The collapse of the communist regimes and socialist economies has brought into surface enormous environmental problems. One of the fields in urgent need of help is the polluting industry which needs to be modernized as the pollution threatens us as well.

The Soviet military bases in the former socialist central eastern European countries have caused immense pollution. In Poland there are large industrialized areas where people suffer from illnesses caused by contamination. In the southern parts of the former German Democratic Republic there are areas where, with minimal safeguards, uranium was produced both for the energy production of the socialist countries and for the Soviet nuclear weapons. In these areas the expected average age is markedly lower than elsewhere in the eastern parts of Germany. In the same regions children's cancer rates are considerably higher than average and the constant radiation causes other illnesses as well.

We know of several environmental catastrophes in the geographical area which we have learned to know as the Soviet Union.[2] The Aral Sea is dying. Close to the Soviet nuclear explosion test seat Semipalatinski there is a town whose population is severely affected by the Soviet nuclear tests. This town does not appear on the official Soviet maps and up to the present there have not been any official records about the catastrophal health conditions of the town. In this region the amount of cancer cases is noticeably higher than average in the former Soviet Union and the children, for example, are not healthy enough to be able to cope with normal school days. This information about the region has been stated in the UN report 'Comprehensive Study on Nuclear Weapons' published in 1990.

In the Kola region as well as in Siberia there are large areas where the forests have either been destroyed by environmental pollution or have been utilized for the Soviet economic development. As a result of these environmental changes many indigenous peoples have lost the economic basis of their life in these regions (Roginko 1992). They have been forced to move into cities and adapt to modern life; at the same time they have lost their cultural identity.

After the collapse of socialism it is easy to blame it for the environmental catastrophes and portray it as a system which destroys its natural environment. While talking about environmental problems caused by socialist systems it is easy to forget that in market economies or in capitalism there also exist severe environmental problems. For example, the acid rain in Norway did not originate in any socialist country but in Great Britain. But this is not the most essential argument here. It is more important to understand that the socialist economic system has in many essential parts been only a bleak copy of the capitalist system. Both economic systems have attempted to generate economic growth in order to increase material wealth. Totalitarian and centralized socialist systems may have been in a better position to brutally exploit nature for the economic benefit of the people, or in fact to reach the material standard of the capitalist world. Socialism has therefore been just as much growth-oriented as the market economies.

In order to show the superiority of the socialist system in comparison to the capitalist one, the socialist regimes were eager to establish large-scale projects. According to Lenin the construction of socialism was tantamount to the electrification of the Soviet Union. Socialism was to signify the modernization of the Soviet Union. In order to produce all the energy needed for industry, huge dams and artificial lakes were constructed. And to increase the food production enormous watering systems were constructed and dry steppe lands were turned into cultivated fields. There seemed to be no need to take nature into account and the projects caused enormous environmental problems. The environment was sacrificed so as to achieve rapid and massive economic growth.

The environmental catastrophes are in no way specific to any social system. In addition to the former socialist countries, large scale environmental catastrophes can be found in the developing countries. Already now there are more environmental than political refugees in the developing world. One of the main reasons for environmental problems of the developing countries has been the modernization project which aims at economic growth (Hettne 1984). The economic, political and social systems of the developing world have been developed according to the Euro-American model. In this modernization model development means particularly economic growth. The growth has been reached by intensifying export-oriented agriculture and by constructing export industries. In developing countries it has been easy to ignore the environmental norms and thus the pursuit of effectiveness and cost-effective production has lead to intensified erosion and pollution.

Even if the sectors related to the world economy have been modernized and are capable of producing growth, the overall national economy of the developing countries has not improved in any significant degree as more than half, in some cases even 80%, of the population earn their living from the traditional sectors of the economy. At the same time the traditional sectors produce less than half of the GNP of the countries concerned.[3] The export-oriented industries undermine the resources and hamper the functioning of these traditional sectors. The diminishing space for subsistence economy has increased the stress on the environment since in order to provide means for daily life people have been forced to utilize marginalized land. It is therefore possible to say that in this case, too, the growth-oriented economy is closely connected to environmental catastrophes.

Severe environmental problems are not only found in the former socialist and underdeveloped world; they are also an inevitable phenomenon in the growth-oriented market economies, i.e. the model which both the East and the West are now striving for. Growth of production and consumption have been closely linked with centralization and urbanization which have both increased ecological stress in the market economies (Adler-Karlsson 1990). The economic growth and the environmental problems of our time are largely inseparable. But this has not prevented experts and politicians, even the Brundtland Report, from talking about sustainable development in connection with growth-oriented economy. In fact, when speaking of sustainable development they actually mean sustainable industrial growth.

In the Brundtland Report sustainable development was already connected with growth. Growth was even seen as a precondition for solving environmental problems (Brundtland Report 1987). This can be compared to the assumption that the problems of the developing countries can only be solved by means of western economic growth. Understood in this way, sustainable development can be accepted by anyone. This is also a neutral and natural science-oriented attitude towards environmental problems and pollution. We are all concerned about the environment. The only way to achieve a consensus like this was to separate environmental problems from economic, political and social orders. Already in the 1960s there was a strong environmental consciousness but at that time the solution for environmental problems was connected to the political and social struggle (Finger 1992).

Today one can say that in the 1960s the solution for environmental problems was connected to socialist revolutions in a very naive way. It was taken almost for granted that socialism automatically creates the basis for solving not only class contradictions but also the contradiction between the social order and the environment. Today we know that socialism was not necessarily any answer. But it is, however, just as naive to exclude economic, political and social struggles from solving the environmental problems. In the frame of the modernization project it is quite natural to see technological development as a key to solving environmental problems and turning to sustainable development. We need cleaner technology and cleaning technology to decrease the stress on ecology.

The faith in technical solutions opens an option for continued growth and increased consumption. The same economic actors which have caused the degradation of the environment now produce new technology for the protection of it. This technology might even become the growth sector of economy and a basis for the future growth. If this is going to be the case, it means that you are first allowed to destroy the environment while making profit and then you may make extra profit by saving or protecting it. To me this sounds a bit schizophrenic. I would therefore like to take up a slightly different perspective.

3. Socialization and Social Philosophy as Sources of Environmental Problems

I am not going to make a long historical journey through the centuries from the traditional societies via great ancient civilizations and feudalism to the present. Still I would like to highlight some historical aspects. We know that most of the traditional societies were small by their population. They lived in various environments from the Arctic to the Saharan deserts and to the rain forests. The economic order of those societies was based on subsistence and the societies used their environment in a sustainable way. Before the age of technological development they had no other alternative.

People in those different societies distant from each other were very similar when it comes to the reproduction of the human species and to the interests and utopias of human dreams. But there was and still is one important factor separating those societies from each other. This factor was culture. Culture has been a social code to adapt the society into very different ecological regions (Sarmela 1989). Culture has also given the norms to use nature in a sustainable way. Today we can utilize our physical environment much more effectively, and cultural codes no longer have the same role as they had in traditional societies. There is a process of cultural harmonization going on in the world on a global scale and we are losing our adaptability (Sarmela 1989).

Tributary societies which followed traditional societies were partly based on technical development and produced surplus. Surplus was produced by a growth-oriented economic order or it was extracted from other societies by violent means. Still up to the 15th century surplus meant a collection of treasures. Growth also gave the surplus needed for armed protection of the wealth created by the society.

Arms were also needed for robbing the wealth of other societies. This indicates that armed security and growth are closely intertwined throughout the history of human kind (Käkönen 1992).

There are hardly any social theories which integrate social systems with natural systems (Lee 1990). On the contrary, there is a long post-Renaissance tradition to strictly separate those two (Connolly 1989). This division is an integral aspect of modern sciences. Before the Renaissance nature was regarded as a more or less holy entity in the European civilization (Connolly 1989). God's works and wisdom could be admired in nature. Man did not have a right to destroy the harmony created by God (Connolly 1990). The social theories of this time used the harmony of nature as a model.

During the Renaissance the harmony was broken. Metaphorically speaking, the Europeans killed their God (Connolly 1989). People gradually revealed God's secrets in nature. Nature was objectivized and it was utilized for human material welfare. During this process the Europeans occupied the position of God and became the masters of nature.

The development of social theories reflected the change described above. One of the main aims of social theories has been to promote material welfare and, in relation to economic growth, also to promote social equality in Europe. Even today the situation is more or less the same. Social theories are connected with economic growth (Hettne 1984). There are no social theories related to zero growth or absolute scarcity of resources and environment.

As parts of the modernization process, industrialization and urbanization changed the relation between people and nature even further. Nature became an object which was to be utilized and also forced under human will. At the same time technological development enabled more and more effective exploitation of nature. The Europeans lost their daily contact with nature and began to view it as a part of a romanticized past — a paradise lost (Connolly 1989). Therefore the norms or rules limiting human activities vis-à-vis nature ceased to exist. The restorability of the biosphere was lost.

The second aspect I will refer to in this article has a long history. In a global scale the human race has traditionally lived in a decentralized system. This is not to say that there have not been any centralized social systems and even civilizations (Sarmela 1989; Adler-Karlsson 1990). But before the 16th century even the centralized systems were parts of a decentralized system and they were more or less regional or local by nature. Therefore it is also difficult to talk about peripheries and centres in a global sense in the pre-Renaissance world (Amin 1989).[4]

In the history of human kind there seems to be a tendency towards centralization. Since the Renaissance the centralization process has accelerated its pace and has been characteristically global (Wallerstein 1987). Improved technical means have made it possible to utilize nature more effectively. This has given an option to go over from the stage of producing for the immediate survival of a human society to the stage of growth of material welfare.

The aspect presented above indicates that centralization and material growth as well as the growth of population are closely interconnected (Adler-Karlsson 1990). One can say that since the Renaissance, European civilization has clearly been growth-oriented. Human and social centralization require more effective production of material goods than a decentralized system. Increased production increases the stress on the natural environment. This chain leads to the conclusion that centralized systems destroy the biosphere and prevent its capability for self-restoration. This has been true also in pre-modern centralized social systems.

According to historical experience the global centralizing system has a tendency to homogenize previously peripheral systems. This takes place in connection with the effective utilization of the peripheries for the benefit of the centres (Sarmela 1989; Wallerstein 1987; Amin 1989). In this process adaptive social systems and civilizations disappear and are replaced by local clones of the centres.

4. The Preconditions for Sustainable Development

The way I have discussed economic growth, environment and sustainable development shows that growth-orientation is based on brutal exploitation of both human beings and nature (Adler-Karlsson 1990). It also means that the way we see the world and understand the social reality is connected with growth. It is not easy to step outside the framework we have internalized in the socialization process. The claim that almost everything we have learned to be good is a source of alienation and environmental disasters is therefore hard to accept. This leads to the conclusion that no real alternative is possible to achieve without changing the way we think and the way we theoretically organize the social reality, without changing both the political and the economic system we live in. Furthermore, it means that environmental problems are in the end social and political by nature.

I would like to use the present Finnish situation as an example of the difficulty of turning one's back to growth-orientation and going towards sustainable development. The economic situation in Finland can be called depression. The Finnish GNP is declining and unemployment is increasing. The rate of unemployment in Finland has already exceeded 15 per cent in 1992. This development has lead to declining consumption and production and thus to diminishing state income. As a result there are less means for a social security policy and all that leads to a further decline in production. We are in a vicious circle, and in the traditional point of view the only way out can be found by increasing export.

The situation is not acceptable in the frames of the values we have. Solutions which would lead back to growth have therefore been the goal of various ruling elites in Finland. Growing economy is still the ultimate goal of the political decision makers. There is no way out of the dilemma. In public debates this attitude can be supported by the argument that the problems of the developing world can not be solved without economic growth. And it is easy to believe that the increase in the standard of living of the majority of the world population is impossible without a huge increase in the industrial and agricultural output. This is certainly true, if our aim is to offer our western level of consumption to the whole of humankind.

But, if we take a critical standpoint, we have to ask whether the OECD standard of living is possible for everyone. How high a growth rate would be needed for the other 80 per cent of the world population to reach our standard of living, let us say, in 20 years? How would it affect the environment? By simple mathematical calculations it is easy to demonstrate that equality on the OECD level is not only utopistic but also impossible. This easily leads towards the idea of selective growth. Economic growth and a high level of consumption is possible only for a limited population. Chosen people or people who have chosen themselves have to protect themselves by military means against the threats of the outside world.

This kind of argumentation leads to the conclusion that sustainable development has to be an alternative for growth-oriented modernization. I will use the above arguments as my starting point for demonstrating the need for an alternative strategy to overcome the crisis of the modernization project.

The demonstration is based on a dichotomic chart presentation. On one dimension there are two mutually exclusive alternative ways of social development, growth-oriented and sustainable development, on the other dimension two security options, armed security and civil security. Armed security is closely interconnected with both economic growth and unified state. By civil security I mean a very wide conception of security which is primarily based on fulfilling basic human needs.

Table 3.1
Four fold of security and development

	Growth-oriented development	Sustainable development
Armed security	A	B
Civil security	C	D

The four fold offers the following alternatives for security: 1) Switch over to sustainable development still preserving the armed security. This proves out to be a dead end and one can only return back to A. Armed security cannot be maintained without economic growth and often effective exploitation of nature; 2) Switch over to civil security within the framework of growth-oriented economy and stop using money on arms. This, too, is a deadlock and leads back to A. In a strongly unequal society maintaining a high standard of consumption for oneself requires armed protection against the others. The more so as it becomes more and more obvious that any attempt to obtain a high standard of living for everyone inevitably leads to catastrophes.

The only alternative thus seems to be switching directly and comprehensively from A to D. In other words, the basic values of the society, and thus the whole complex social reality, have to be changed. Partial solutions will only lead to serious catastrophes. Even so, it is worth pointing out that a conscious and determined policy can in principle enable moving directly from A to D or through the phases of B or C.

This demonstration supports the idea that sustainable development is only thinkable in a decentralized social system. As far as this is true we have to ask whether it is possible to turn away from the current centralizing development before any major catastrophes occur. Briefly, I would like to add that an alternative calls for local democracy which is connected to civil society. This requires a new definition of democracy since the way we understand democracy is closely connected to unified state and economic growth. A decentralized future also presupposes adaptive utilization of nature. This requires a new definition of development and social welfare. And global equality can only be reached by the policy of giving up the OECD standard of living. All this requires a new kind of social philosophy as well as new kinds of social theories.

Notes

1. See for instance 'Report on the state of the environment in the USSR 1988'. USSR State Committee for protection of Nature, Moscow 1989.
2. See the note above.
3. See for instance the statistics in the World Development Report 1992.
4. There are also scholars like Andre Gunder Frank who argue that since the great Mesopotamian civilizations the world system has been the same by its basic structure. That means that there have been peripheries and centres. And the centre of the system has moved westwards. These ideas Frank presented for instance in the ISA Conference in Atlanta, 31 March - 4 April 1992.

References

Adler-Karlsson, Gunnar, 1990. *90-luvun oppikirja.* Jyväskylä: Art House.
Amin, Samir, 1989. *Eurocentrism.* London: Zed Books.
'Brundtland Report', 1987. Yhteinen tulevaisuutemme. Ympäristön ja kehityksen maailmankomission raportti. Ulkoasiainministeriö, Ympäristöministeriö. Helsinki: Valtion painatuskeskus.
Comprehensive Study on Nuclear Weapons, 1990. Department for Disarmament, United Nations, New York.
Connolly, William E., 1989. *Political Theory and Modernity.* Oxford and New York: Basil Blackwell.
Finger, Matthias, 1991. 'New Horizons for Peace Research: the Global Environment', in Jyrki Käkönen (ed.), *Perspectives on Environmental Conflict and International Politics.* London and New York: Pinter Publishers.
Hettne, Björn, 1984. Development Theory and the Third World. Sarec Report R2:1982, Helsingborg.
Lee, Keekok, 1989. *Social Philosophy and Ecological Scarcity.* London and New York: Routledge.
Roginko, Alexei Y., 1992. 'Conflict between Environment and Development in the Soviet Arctic', in Jyrki Käkönen (ed.), *Vulnerable Arctic: Need for an Alternative?* Tampere Peace Research Institute, Research Report, No. 47, 1992, Tampere.
Sarmela, Matti, 1989. *Rakennemuutos tulevaisuuteen.* Porvoo, Helsinki, Juva: WSOY.
Wallerstein, Immanuel, 1987. *Historiallinen kapitalismi.* Jyväskylä: Vastapaino.
World Development Report 1992. Development and the Environment. The International Bank for Reconstruction and Development. Oxford University Press.

4 Arctic development, environment and northern natives in Russia

Alexei Yu. Roginko

1. Evolvement of the Soviet Arctic Policy

For obvious reasons, the Arctic region has always played a special role for the Soviet Union as well as for Russia. Russia is by far the largest of all the Arctic rim nations. Roughly half the land area of the Circumpolar North lies within Russia, and this land area in turn constitutes half of the territory of the country. Out of the 12 million people inhabiting the Circumpolar area, 10 million live in Russia. Historically, the dominant factors determining the USSR Arctic policy have been the military-strategic and the economic ones. The latter has been tied almost exclusively to the development of abundant mineral and fossil fuel resources in the area. The priority of the military factor in using the spaces of the Arctic can be explained in terms of international relations in the region, which long before World War II (and since the beginning of the Cold War in particular) has become involved into the sphere of military confrontation between the two opposing 'socio-economic systems'. As a result, the Arctic has been viewed in the USSR primarily in the light of strategic interests, and cooperation in economic, scientific and environmental fields has been accorded secondary, if any, priority.

The Murmansk initiative forwarded by President M. Gorbachev in October 1987, marked a turning point in the Soviet Arctic policies. The most striking feature of the initiative was that it represented an authoritative exposition of a unified approach to Arctic policy by the Soviet Union, bringing together security, resource, scientific and environmental issues. It reflected an idea of broadening the concept of international security, of a close interconnection between its civil and military elements, an understanding that economic development and environmental protection are both, in considerable measure, contingent upon controlling the arms race.

Since the time of the Murmansk speech, more has been done by the Soviet Union to develop Arctic cooperation on an international arena than throughout the previous 70 years. The Arctic region has been accorded one of the highest priorities in the Soviet foreign policy in general. But, what is probably even more important, the Murmansk initiatives could not but have a profound impact on the domestic dimension of the Soviet Arctic policy, radically changing the order of priorities in the use of Arctic resources and space. What is the essence of these changes? First of all, it is the realization of the need for Arctic policy to serve a variety of interests. If it was previously designed to address primarily strategic resource and, to a certain extent, scientific concerns, the contemporary approach is marked by a clear-cut shift of priorities towards the social domain. A whole complex of military, environmental, scientific, economic and social factors is taken into account while formulating the current Russian Arctic policies. A drastic increase in the importance of a socio-environmental sphere, accompanied by a relative reduction in the weight of strategic problems, have resulted in a certain levelling of various policy issues significance. But the existing possibilities of dealing with each of them, the experience already acquired as well as the extent of their neglect vary substantially. Of particular concern today are the environmental issues and the whole complex of problems related to the needs and interests of the northern native peoples (see Vartanov & Roginko 1990).

2. Conflict Between Environment and Economic Development

For decades, the Soviet economic policy and practice in the use of Arctic resources and spaces were dominated by the attitude which can be formulated as follows: "the more we take from the Arctic, the better". And when there emerged contradictions concerning different uses of the Arctic, or between environmental and social priorities, on the one hand, and resource development, on the other, this issue was, as a rule, resolved to the detriment of the former. For a long time all economic activities in the North have been (and still mostly are) exclusively resource-oriented. Still, the Soviet Union relies heavily on the Arctic for the supply of fossil-fuel resources: the Siberian Arctic accounts for almost two thirds of national oil and more than 60 per cent of natural gas production, and these percentages are bound to increase substantially, especially when the Arctic offshore oil and gas development starts.

Such an approach to the development of the Soviet North has resulted in a deep conflict between the economic interests of the industrial civilization and the Arctic ecosystems which are now functioning at critical levels. And what is even more important, it is the interests, the identity, and the very existence of small northern aboriginal peoples which are now at risk. The few improvements that industrial civilization and technology have brought about into the life of northern natives are far outweighed by the damage inflicted upon the Arctic environment by the ministries, agencies and organizations conducting practically unregulated and uncontrolled large-scale industrial development.

Reckless, aggressive exploitation of the northern environment by the Soviet industrial ministries undermined the natural basis of small indigenous peoples' existence. Being forcefully resettled into small towns, they are gradually losing their traditions of reindeering, hunting and fishing; as a rule, they occupy the lowest rungs of the social status ladder. Their human environment, material culture and social organization are being changed so drastically that it is difficult to guarantee their survival in the coming decades. The destruction of the traditional life-style results in unemployment, high criminal and suicide rates, alcoholism, etc. The average life expectancy is comparable only to that in the least developed countries 43-45 years for men, about 55 years for women. Infant mortality has also been exceptionally high (see Pika & Prokhorov 1988; Golubchikov 1989). Several of the 26 small northern aboriginal peoples even decreased in number during the decade of the 1980s. And this is not an effect of a certain universal process dooming any small peoples to extinction, as some would seem to suggest, but rather a direct result of an incompetent social policy. To cite just one fact, while back in the 1960s average life expectancies of North American Inuits and Soviet northern natives were roughly equal (62 years), two decades later the same index has increased by about 10 years on the one side of the Bering Strait, and decreased by 10-15 years on the other one (Sangi 1990).

What is most important to realize is that no comprehensive solution of any pressing issues concerning the northern aboriginal peoples can be achieved without the active involvement of the northern natives themselves. Any attempts to implement any, even most helpful, measures from "above" from Moscow or Tyumen, from Magadan or Krasnoyarsk are doomed to fail. The independence of their development is the only possible means of their survival, because if the barrier of social passivity and alienation is not broken by the natives themselves, no support from outside will help. What the central authorities should do is to curb the expansion of industrial ministries to the North, to make them respect and consider the needs and interests of aboriginal peoples. It should be left for the natives themselves to decide what is better for them traditionalism or industrial development, reindeer or oil, privileges from the state or economic prospects (Pika & Prokhorov 1988).

Up to the present day, the role of the local authorities in the regions of new industrial development has been negligible, and the opinion of native peoples has been ignored by the industrial agencies exploiting the northern environment. Now the situation is gradually changing. The new union and republican laws have granted the northern communities new rights and they are now able to dispose of the cooperative property on their lands and resources more or less independently. But local authorities and executive bodies have little experience of this kind, and they are faced with strong opposition of the industrial circles. Although the latter are now under heavy pressure of public and scientific organizations, the ministries and their enterprises are still trying to mitigate the claims of environmentalists and native peoples. The relations between the local authorities and the industry should be based on leasing agreements with appropriate payments for territory, natural resources, and reimbursement of environmental damage (Andreyeva 1991).

At the end of March 1990, the first Congress of peoples of the North was held, and the Association of Small Northern Peoples was established. Its aims are the promotion of political, social and economic rights of the northern natives, preservation of their cultural identity, control over resource exploitation in the territories of their residence, as well as the representation of these peoples' interests at all governmental levels. In the declaration adopted by the Congress, its participants called for a revision of principles of northern territories' industrial development; they demanded, in particular, that any large-scale project concerning utilization of natural resources should undergo the examination of the relevant regional native peoples' associations (*Izvestiya* 1990, No. 92).

There is now some hope that the demands of the northern peoples will have better chances of being realized in the coming years than previously. A completely new concept of social and economic development of the northern peoples themselves (and not just the areas of their habitation) up to the year 2005 is now being realized. A new structure within the Russian Government State Commission on Socio-Economic Development of the North has been established in June 1990. According to the current plans, 6.4 billion rubles are to be spent during the five-year period (1991-1995) to meet the vital needs of the northern natives, including their traditional trades development, health, education, and housing construction.

At the same time, a significant element of uncertainty has been introduced into the situation with socio-economic development and environmental protection in the North by the call by former Soviet republics for increased local control over resources as well as the authority necessary for their management. The parliament of the Russian Federation (RSFSR) has declared its property rights for all the resources found in its territories, and moreover, the same thing has been done by most of the national-territorial formations within the RSFSR (autonomous republics, autonomous districts etc.). Much of the legal responsibility for environmental protection in Russia (particularly with respect to the North), and perhaps more importantly, the resources for adequate management and enforcement, presently rests with central authorities. This presents a dilemma in terms of who would manage environmental protection programs and how effectively management could be accomplished in the event that the republics were able to press their claims. Many of the experts in the country doubt whether the autonomous republics like Chukotka or even Yakutia are able to adequately manage their vast territories, to develop natural resources, to protect the environment, and to provide huge investments necessary for social programs, infrastructure, etc., independently, without the support of the centre. The Far North is the territory of national, all-union significance, and to develop it, state investments and state programs are required (Krasnopolski 1991).

3. Possible Solutions

The northern regions of the RSFSR comprise today the largest remaining territorial and environmental reserve of the country and of mankind in general. Vast expanses of tundra, forest tundra, and taiga play a prominent role in supplying mankind with atmospheric oxygen, in regulating the environmental balance in the whole of the Northern hemisphere. Thus the North is perhaps even more important not as a supplier of raw materials and fuel, but as a reserve of unoccupied areas which in the present conditions of increasing explosive hazards of a technosphere becomes particularly necessary. Therefore, at least theoretically, we should be interested in keeping the northern spaces as intact as possible. But we have to be realistic. Today one can hardly speak of the North's total conservation even though such ideas were widely spread in the USA and Canada some 10-15 years ago. Of course, we need the North's resources and they will have to be developed. At the same time, the need for conservation of these resources, for preserving the northern environment is becoming ever more obvious. It is even more obvious that there exist alternatives for the North's resources, at least for their larger part. Resource-saving measures, reducing raw materials and energy consumption and the use of various substitutes will undoubtedly bring about a dramatic decrease in the exploitation of many sources of fuel and raw materials, including those available in the North. That is why the search for alternatives to the northern resources can be viewed today as a major way of reducing the anthropogenous and technogenic impact on the North, particularly the Arctic, which is most vulnerable in terms of environmental damage (Agranat & Andreyeva 1990).

Apart from that, several other measures of a broad economic character can be suggested as a means of restructuring the economy of the Russian North and hence of reducing deleterious human impact on the Arctic environment. Among them are the following:
- re-orientation of the foreign trade structure towards a decrease in unprocessed fuel exports share;
- raising the efficiency of resources and particularly oil extraction (at present the oil stratum output rate does not exceed 40 percent);
- revision of resource prices to include an element covering the 'post-resource' development and environmental damage;

- revision of approaches to the complex industrial development in the northern environmental conditions: is there always a need to build up a superstructure of deep processing of the extracted raw materials?
- gradual diversification of economic specialization to include the non-resource types of economic activities: recreation, tourism, transportation and transit (including intercontinental) functions; revival of the traditional industries of the indigenous population (see Shlikhter 1990).

In addition to economic measures, a whole range of specific legislative and administrative steps is required to resolve the complex issues regarding interrelations between economic development and environmental protection in the Arctic.

First, radical modification of production location schemes is necessary: the northern environment may not sustain such a congestion of industrial enterprises which the mid-latitude areas until recently coped with fairly well. Huge enterprises and territorial-industrial complexes prove to be literally ravishing the environment of the Arctic. For instance, in the Kola Peninsula emissions of sulphur are twice as great as those in the whole of Finland. The so-called industrial desert in this region with practically no living plants covers an area of about 100,000 hectares. The area where sulphur deposition is estimated to be 1-2 grams per square meter annually amounts to about 5 mln. hectares, approximately half the size of Finnish Lapland; on that area trees are defoliated and changes in the composition of lichen and moss species are observed (Varmola 1989). In the regions around Norilsk, vegetation cover is virtually destroyed in the areas covering several hundred of square kilometers: within the radius of 100 km from the city, concentrations of copper in snow cover and moss amount to 40-70 mg/kg, and those of nickel to 400 mg/kg (*Nauka i Zhizn* 1990, No. 10). Hence, ways of maximum possible decentralization of industry in the North, where the assimilative capacity of the environment is subaverage, should be explored. There are even suggestions to suspend temporarily all the industrial development in the Arctic and to concentrate the efforts on the development central regions (see Kotlyakov & Agranat 1989).

Any legislative and administrative instruments regulating economic activities in the North should be specifically suited to the ecological and geographical conditions of this region, low temperatures, permafrost and general instability of geoecological systems. For instance, the introduction of specific emission and pollutants' load standards, more stringent as compared to mid-latitudes, is urgently required in the Arctic. Penalties and sanctions for the breach of nature protection laws and regulations should also be much stricter bearing in mind that the restoration of the disturbed environment here might take centuries. Legal measures aimed at protecting the Arctic environment should provide not only for the compensation of environmental damage costs but for the prevention of such damage itself.

This, in turn, necessitates the development of a new system for assessing land and natural resources' value in the North which must take into account potential environmental damage costs. This system should be based not on the use of the resources visible presently or in the near future, but on the experts' assessments of the importance of the North's ecosystems and its riches in the long run. Otherwise we would come to the conclusion that, say, dwarf willows or birches are "worth" nothing (Agranat & Andreyeva 1990). The losses due to one ruined hectare of the tundra and forest-tundra amount to no more than 2-3 thousand rubles if calculated according to the currently accepted methods (mainly the losses of reindeer-breeding and hunting economy). For comparison, similar losses in the developed and populated forest-steppe zones in the South of Russia are estimated at 50-60 thousand rubles. But if we take into account the costs of northern ecosystems' rehabilitation, the damage estimated might increase hundreds of times, or even become infinitely high, since the ruined ecosystems in the Arctic might be irrevocably lost.

One cannot say that nothing is being done in the field of Arctic environmental protection legislation in the Soviet Union. Good laws are being passed, but their provisions remain mainly on paper, not being enforced. For example, in November 1984 the Decree of the Presidium of the Supreme Soviet was passed, named "On the strengthening of nature protection in the regions of High North and sea areas adjacent to the northern coast of the USSR". It envisaged the establishment of a network of natural reserves, placed strict limitations on the use of transport, tourism and industrial development in the Arctic, provided for special design, equipment and manning standards for vessels operating in the Arctic waters, for the establishment of periods of time as well as specific sea areas closed for navigation, etc. (see *Vedomosti Verkhovnogo Soveta SSSR* 1984, No. 48). But the problem is that the concrete norms and rules upon which the implementation and enforcement of the Decree depend were not elaborated for years. The ministries and agencies involved have been blocking the issue. A complex of measures designed to expedite the implementation of the Decree has been provided for by the special Enactment of the USSR Council of Ministers passed in 1990, six years after the Decree itself. According to the text of the Enactment, relevant draft norms and rules should have been prepared by the agencies involved within three months (see *Sobraniye Postanovleniy Pravitel'stva SSSR* 1990, No. 16). But still, in the spring of 1991 this task remains unfulfilled.

Finally, one more issue of direct relevance to the effectiveness of the Arctic environmental policy in Russia is that of funding. Environment protection in the High North is a costly undertaking indeed. And if there is one country whose Arctic environment is most heavily degraded and who at the same time is desperately in need of additional funds for meeting the vital basic needs of its population, it is Russia. In the current conditions funding for new national commitments to Arctic environmental protection will be most certainly hard to find in Russia. Russia is in grave need of advanced and environment-friendly technology, to say nothing of the clean-up and restorative actions in its part of the Arctic. Therefore effective domestic action for Arctic environmental protection will require not only scientific and technical cooperation on the part of the other Arctic and Nordic states but new economic relations between the Western countries and Russia which entail a net transfer of resources to the latter (see Griffiths & Young 1990).

References

Agranat G. A. and Andreyeva E. N. , 1990. 'Priority Economic, Technological and Ecological Problems of International Scientific Cooperation in the North', in *Arctic Research: Advances and Prospects*. Proceedings of the Conference of Arctic and Nordic Countries on Coordination of Research in the Arctic, Leningrad, December 1988. Part 2, pp. 399-407. Moscow: Nauka.
Andreyeva E., 1991. 'Oil and Gas Development in the North: Social and Environmental Conflict Analysis'. A paper presented at NAS/AS USSR Workshop on Cooperation in Arctic/Northern Social Science, Moscow, April 7-11, 1991 (mimeo).
Golubchikov Yu., 1989. 'Losing second Alaska', *Sovetskava Kultura*, July 13 [in Russian].
Griffiths F. and Young, O. R., 1990. *Protecting the Arctic's Environment: Impressions of the Co-chairs*. Hanover: Working Group on Arctic International Relations (Reports and Papers; 1990-1).
Kotlyakov V. and Agranat, G., 1989. 'Tropics of the North', *Pravda*, May 9 [in Russian].
Krasnopolski B. Kh., 1991. 'Scientific Cooperation in the Field of Socio-Economic Research of the Arctic and the North'. A paper presented at NAS/AS USSR Workshop on Cooperation in Arctic/Northern Social Science, Moscow, April 7-11, 1991 (mimeo).
Nauka i Zhizn, 1990, No. 10, p. 109.
Pika A. and Prokhorov, B., 1988. 'Large problems of small peoples', *Kommunist*, No. 16, pp. 76-83 [in Russian].
Sangi V., 1990. 'To return rights to the owners of the land', *Izvestiva*, July 12 [in Russian].
Shlikhter S. B., 1990. 'Present-Day Problems of Economic Development of the North', in *Arctic Research: Advances and Prospects*. Proceedings of the Conference of Arctic and Nordic Countries on Coordination of Research in the Arctic, Leningrad, December 1988. Part 2, pp. 419-21. Moscow: Nauka.
Sobraniye Postanovleniv Pravitel'stva SSSR, 1990, No. 16, st. 87.
Varmola M., 1989. 'The state of forests in Finnish Lapland'. A background paper prepared for the Consultative Meeting on the Protection of the Arctic Environment, Rovaniemi, September 20-26 1989 (mimeo).

Vartanov R. V. and Roginko, A. Yu., 1990. 'New Dimensions of Soviet Arctic Policy: Views from the Soviet Union', *Annals of the American Academy of Political and Social Sciences*, Vol. 512, November, pp. 69-78.
Vedomosti Verkhovnogo Soveta SSSR, 1984, No. 48, st. 863.

5 Arctic haze: an exploration of international regime alternatives

Marvin S. Soroos

1. Introduction

Nearly a century ago, Fridtjof Nansen observed dark stains on the polar ice that he believed were caused by airborne pollutants (Ottar 1989, p. 2349). Nevertheless, it was generally presumed until recent decades that the air over the Arctic was virtually pristine in view of the sparse population of the region and its geographical isolation from the concentrations of population and industry in the temperate latitudes far to the South.

The first modern indications that Arctic air may not be pure came from a climatologist named J. Murray Mitchell, Jr. While aboard the Ptarmigan weather reconnaissance flights during the 1950s, he observed puzzling patches of haze that significantly reduced atmospheric visibility over the Arctic, (Mitchell 1957). At the time, he did not attribute the phenomenon to human sources and thus did not investigate it further. The haze was rediscovered in 1972 by Glenn E. Shaw, a scientist from the University of Alaska, when he was taking what he thought would be unremarkable measurements of the composition of Arctic air over Point Barrow (Carey 1988).

Shaw's observations triggered substantial research activity on the phenomenon of Arctic haze. In fifteen years, scientists have learned much about the composition of the haze, its seasonal variations, and the origins of the pollutants that cause it. However, significant uncertainties remain on the impacts of the haze on the fragile ecosystems of the Arctic and the possibility that it could be a cause of climate changes within the region and globally.[1]

Despite its potentially significant environmental consequences, the Arctic haze phenomenon has been virtually ignored in international policy circles. This paper offers several explanations for this lack of an international response, then examines eight types of international institutional arrangements, otherwise known as regimes, through which the problem could be addressed. Finally, it looks more closely at the potential of two regime types that are currently active possibilities for mitigating the haze problem. One would extend the relatively well established long-range transboundary air pollution (LRTAP) regime sponsored by the United Nations Economic Commission for Europe. The other would be an outgrowth of the Arctic Environment Protection Strategy adopted by the eight Arctic rim states at a ministerial meeting in Rovaniemi, Finland, in 1991.

2. Arctic Haze and Its Consequences

Systematic scientific investigation of the haze phenomenon began in 1976 with the analysis of air samples collected both from aircraft and at ground level. Over the years, a relatively small community of scientists from several disciplines, in particular atmospheric chemists and aquatic and terrestrial ecologists, have coordinated their research efforts and shared their findings through the periodic meetings of an informal organization known as the Arctic Chemical Network, which was set up in Oslo in May 1977.[2] A program of aircraft sampling has been carried out every third year by the Arctic Gas and Aerosol Sampling Project (AGASP) sponsored by the United States National Oceanic and Atmospheric Administration (NOAA) with the participation of scientists from several countries.

Haze is a mixture of gases and particles that are suspended in air, or what is referred to by scientists as an aerosol (National Research Council 1979, p. 1). The haze found generally over the Arctic region is largely a seasonal phenomenon lasting from November until April, with March being the peak month, when aerosol levels are 20 to 40 times higher than in summer (Barrie 1986, p. 643). Even during its peak during the winter, Arctic haze is not as dense as the smog observed over New York or Los Angeles, but it is more than twenty times as thick as the haze occurring over the more remote Antarctic region (Rahn 1979, p. 8).

The relatively thin haze over the region in the summer is composed largely of natural substances, in particular wind blown dust and sea salt. The much thicker haze of the winter season is comprised primarily of pollutants from human activities, including sulfates, graphitic carbon, organic compounds from pesticides and fungicides, and traces of almost every pollution element found at mid-latitudes, such as mercury, lead, and vanadium (see Barrie 1986, p. 6; Barrie et al., 1991).

Scientists have identified the sources of haze in the Arctic by measuring the relative concentrations of various trace elements, or what are known as the chemical "signatures" of the air. These signatures can be compared to the distinctive composition of pollutants emitted in various regions both inside and outside of the Arctic region. The paths over which these pollutants flow can then be charted using data on seasonal air circulation patterns (Rahn and Shaw 1982; Rahn 1984). By these techniques, it has been determined that almost all of the pollutants causing the winter haze over the Arctic, even over the Alaskan region, originate in the heavily industrialized regions of Europe and the Soviet Union. A relatively small volume of pollutants reaches the Arctic from the North American and East Asian regions (Barrie, Olson and Oikawa 1989).

Meteorological factors are primarily responsible for the greater density of the haze in the winter season. The prevailing Eurasian wind flow in summer is southeast, but in winter it shifts strongly to the northeast. During winter, the seasonal low pressure areas occurring over Europe combine with persistent high pressure over Siberia to trigger strong air "surges" that transport large quantities of polluted air from the European continent thousands of kilometers into the Arctic (Barrie 1986, pp. 647-8). Once pollutants enter the very cold and stable winter Arctic air mass, they are less efficiently dispersed and removed than elsewhere and thus cause the haze phenomenon. During the other seasons, clouds and precipitation scrub most pollutants out of the air before they reach the Arctic region (Heintzenberg et al., 1985, p. 153).

While many of the scientific questions about the density, composition, and sources of Arctic haze now been answered, less is known definitively about the potential environmental impacts of Arctic haze. The effect of the haze on the Arctic region may to some extent be mitigated by wind currents that carry a sizable portion of the aerosols back out of the region (Barrie et al., forthcoming). Nevertheless, there are several reasons for concern that the haze might have serious environmental consequences not only within the Arctic region, but also globally.

Aside from its impact on visibility in the Arctic atmosphere, two principal types of effects of the haze are the primary causes of concern. The first is the damage that the deposition of toxic substances can reek on delicate Arctic ecosystems, in particular the acids that are formed when sulphur constituents combine with moisture either in the air or on the Earth's surface. Acidification can significantly damage terrestrial and aquatic life, especially where the soil is poorly buffered. Lichens, a food of reindeer, are especially vulnerable to increased acidity. The deposition and accumulation of other man-made pollutants, including chlorinated industrial organics, pesticides, and metals such as lead and cadmium, can be highly disruptive to the relatively short food chains that exist in the harsh conditions of the Arctic region (Barrie 1986).

Another potentially significant consequence of the haze is climate change through its impact on radiation balances. Sooty carbon present in the haze not only absorbs solar radiation, but also traps long-range waves reflected from white surfaces such as snow and ice, which could result in a significant warming of the troposphere over the Arctic. Snow and ice cover may be less extensive in a warmer climate, although greater precipitation may be a compensating factor. Carbon particles may also darken the otherwise white surface of snow and ice, thus reducing its albedo, or reflectivity. As more solar energy is absorbed, the rate of the melting will increase (Rahn 1984; Barrie 1986).

Changes in snow and ice cover may trigger additional climatic changes within and beyond the region and contribute to the tendency toward rising sea levels globally. Warmer conditions would cause the permafrost line to recede deeper into the ground, which would reduce moisture levels in the tundra. Fauna and flora inhabiting the region may not be able to survive these changes in their habitat; other species may migrate into the region and take advantage of the less harsh climatic conditions (Maxwell and Barrie 1989, p. 48).

Scientific research on these consequences of Arctic haze is still largely inconclusive. There are reasons to believe that the phenomenon could bring about substantial changes within the region that would in turn have a global impact on climate and sea levels. It is still also possible, however, that the impact of the haze will appear to be insignificant when compared to other environmental changes caused by human activities.

3. Absence of an International Response to Arctic Haze

Rather than developing a comprehensive strategy for preserving the natural environment of the planet as a whole, the international community of states typically responds to specific environmental problems through a wide variety of institutional arrangements of bilateral, regional, and global scope. International regimes and public policies are in place that address a diverse array of environmental problems with varying degrees of success, but many others have received little or no attention among international policy makers.

In general, marine environmental problems have been addressed much more extensively at the international level than have atmospheric ones. Of the 140 agreements appearing in the United Nations Environment Programme's registry of multilateral treaties on the environment, roughly 60 were adopted to conserve fisheries, preserve marine habitats, and reduce pollution from vessel and land-based sources. By contrast, fewer than ten agreements address problems related to the atmosphere (UNEP 1989).

The record on responding to atmospheric problems is also mixed. The Partial Test-Ban Treaty of 1963 provides a blueprint for eliminating radioactive pollution from nuclear weapons testing. A bold regime designed to preserve the stratospheric ozone layer is embodied in the Vienna Convention of 1985, the Montreal Protocol of 1987, and the London Amendments to the protocol of 1990 (see Benedict 1991). A series of agreements on long-range transboundary air pollution, otherwise known as LRTAP, seeks to lessen the acid rain problem in the European and North American regions. Only in 1991 did official negotiations begin on a framework agreement as the first step in an international effort to mitigate global warming caused by the buildup of greenhouse gases in the atmosphere, most notably carbon dioxide.

No international public policy has been adopted for the specific purpose of reducing Arctic haze, nor has a solution to the problem even been the subject of significant multilateral negotiations. What accounts for the lack of an international response to the problem? Let us consider four potential explanations.

The first is the incomplete state of scientific knowledge on the haze phenomenon, in particular on the consequences of the haze. As was noted in the preceding section, Arctic haze has been studied systematically for less than two decades, during which questions about the composition and origin of the haze have largely been answered. However, without definitive evidence that the haze is causing serious damage to the Arctic environment or triggering significant climate changes that could have global impacts, policy makers are unlikely to give priority to mitigating it, especially when other problems, environmental and otherwise, seem to be much more pressing. It may take a surprise revelation, comparable to the discovery of the Antarctic ozone hole, to alter these priorities.

A second potential problem is the remoteness of the Arctic region. The haze problem impacts directly on an area that is very lightly populated, primarily by scattered communities of indigenous peoples in seven of the Arctic rim states (Osherenko and Young 1989). The exception is the Russian Kola Peninsula where there are military installations and large smelting operations.

While indigenous peoples are deeply concerned about the ways in which modern industrial societies infringe upon their environment and way of life, they are hardly in a position to mount much political pressure for action on threats to their welfare, such as Arctic haze. Even with the establishment of the Inuit Circumpolar Conference, which has become a mechanism for making their concerns known to the outside world, the indigenous peoples continue to be marginal participants in international diplomatic processes.

For the much larger populations in the temperate latitudes where most of the pollutants originate, the problem of Arctic haze is largely "out of sight, and out of mind". By contrast, being well aware of the consequences of acid rain on the forests and cities of their region, these populations have strongly demanded action to address the acidification problem, which has taken the form of the LRTAP regime.

Cold War tensions between East and West and the strategic importance of the Arctic region are a third explanation for the lack of an international response to Arctic haze. For decades, scientific research on the Arctic environment was severely hampered by the strategic sensitivities of the superpowers. Scientists were denied access to large parts of the Arctic region and much of the research that was done was classified because of its potential bearing on military operations (Østreng 1989, pp. 102-3). The situation changed considerably when

Soviet President Mikhail Gorbachev, in a speech in Murmansk in 1987, made a strong call for international cooperation on preserving the Arctic environment and promised greater Soviet openness on research in the area (Roginko 1989).

A fourth potential explanation is the assymmetrical relationship between the states that cause the haze problem and the ones that are directly affected by it. The Soviet Union, now Russia, is the only state that is both a substantial contributor to, and victim of, the haze phenomenon. The other Arctic rim states – Norway, Sweden, Finland, Iceland, Canada, and the United States – emit a very small proportion of the pollutants causing the haze. The heavily industrialized European countries to the south, where the haze-forming pollutants originate, are largely unaffected by the haze, but would bear most of the cost of mitigating the problem. Thus, they have little incentive for entering into international agreements on the haze problem.

None of these explanations individually offers a fully persuasive explanation of the lack of an international response to the Arctic haze phenomenon. Inconclusive scientific evidence on the consequences of acid rain and the severity of the threat of ozone depletion did not preclude the adoption of framework conventions on these problems in 1979 and 1985, respectively. A fairly well developed international regime exists for the Antarctic region, despite its even greater remoteness from the major population centers. In fact, because of its distance, Antarctica has been of relatively little strategic interest to the superpowers, which explains their willingness to be unusually cooperative in addressing environmental threats to the region.

Furthermore, strategic sensitivities aside, the Cold War has not prevented environmental cooperation between East and West, but in fact may have had the opposite effect of facilitating it. In the 1970s the superpowers viewed environmental cooperation as a promising ground for reducing East-West tensions, as evidenced by a bilateral agreement on such cooperation concluded between the United States and Soviet Union in 1972 and their participation in the negotiation of the Polar Bear Treaty of 1973. A provision of the 1975 Helsinki Accord calling for East–West cooperation on matters such as energy, transport, and environment led to negotiation of the 1979 LRTAP treaty (Jackson 1990).

Finally, assymmetries between those who cause and are the victims of environmental problems have not always prevented international cooperation. There are instances of upstream riparian states, such as those of the Rhine basin, accepting responsibility for limiting pollution of river systems in deference to the interests of downstream states. In a more general sense, there is a widely accepted tenet of international environmental law, expressed in the often-cited Article 21 of the Declaration adopted at the 1972 Stockholm conference, that states have a responsibility "to ensure that activities within their jurisdiction or control do not cause damage to the environment of other States or of areas beyond the limits of national jurisdiction" (UN Conference on the Human Environment 1972).

Thus, there is no simple explanation for why so little has been done thus far to address the Arctic haze problem. Historical experience in addressing other problems suggests that no one of the four factors alone constitutes an insurmountable obstacle to international cooperation. The lack of an international response to the haze problem should be understood as a combination of these factors.

4. Regime Alternatives for Addressing Arctic Haze

The problem of Arctic haze could be addressed in a variety of institutional contexts, which can be distinguished both by the range of problems that they address and by the geographical scope of the participating states. Turning first to range of function, the haze problem could be taken up by a regime that focuses on a) the haze problem exclusively, b) transboundary air pollution generally, c) a broader variety of environmental problems, or d) a wider array of environmental and non-environmental issues. The geographical scope of the regime could be a) limited to the eight Arctic rim states or b) involve states from beyond the region as part of an inter-regional or global arrangement.

The eight potential regime configurations are presented in Table 5.1. Let us consider each of these alternatives noting environmental regimes having similar combinations of functional and geographical scope that can serve as models for each possibility.

Table 5.1
International Regime Alternatives for Addressing Arctic Haze

	Geographical Scope	
Breadth of Function	Arctic Rim	Interregional/Global
Haze Exclusively	I	II
Transboundary Air Pollution	III	IV
Environment Generally	V	VI
Comprehensive (inc. non-environmental)	VII	VIII

The first two regime types are the most narrowly focused in addressing Arctic haze exclusively. Regime type I would be limited to restricting the emission of haze causing pollutants among the Arctic rim states. In these respects, it would resemble the 1973 Agreement on the Conservation of Polar Bears, adhered to by Canada, Denmark, Norway, the USSR, and the USA, which has proven to be quite successful in fulfilling its limited objectives. An Arctic haze regime of such restricted membership would not be as effective because it would not engage the states that generate most of the haze causing pollutants.

Regime type II would also focus narrowly on the task of limiting the pollutants responsible for the haze, but draw in other states, presumably the eastern and western European ones primarily responsible for the problem. The 1989 Convention on Control of Transboundary Movements of Hazardous Wastes is a prototype of such a type II regime in establishing a partnership between the exporters and importers of toxic wastes. If it can be negotiated, such a regime can be an effective way of addressing a problem. Finding grounds for an agreement may be difficult, however, because the narrow range of issues provides few possibilities for mutually advantageous tradeoffs between the exporters and importers of the air pollutants.

The next two regime alternatives would have a broader focus, but nevertheless be restricted to a certain type of environmental problem, such as transboundary air pollution. The various regional seas programs, the most prominent being the Med Plan that seeks to pollution of the Mediterranean Sea, have the attributes of a type III regime (see Haas 1990). Thus, in addition to haze causing pollutants, a type III response to the haze problem might regulate other pollutants which drift across the boundaries of the Arctic states, including emissions from the large nickel smelters of the Russian Kola peninsula that have been of concern to Finland and Norway.

The 1973 Convention on International Trade in Endangered Species is an example of a type IV regime in that it was established to preserve endangered species generally, not a single one such as the polar bear or fur seal. It also has the participation of a large number of states, including both importers and exporters of live specimens or products from these species.

Regime types III and IV have proven to be effective mechanisms for addressing numerous international environmental problems. They are still narrowly enough focused to stimulate a response to a specific problem, while offering more possibilities for tradeoffs among participating states with divergent interests than do the first two alternatives.

The next two regime types deal with a wide range of environmental problems, but not any other issue areas. While there would seem to be many advantages to addressing the interrelated environmental problems of a region in a comprehensive or holistic manner, such an approach has rarely been adopted multilaterally. The regional seas regimes address a variety of types and sources of marine pollution, but do not fit into this category because their mandate does not encompass other environmental problems, such as regulating the harvesting of fisheries. The agreement on environmental protection that was adopted in 1974 by four Scandinavian or Nordic countries – Norway, Sweden, Finland, and Denmark – might be considered a type V regime. However, it is limited rather narrowly to providing redress for victims of environment damaging activities taking place in one of the other states and, thus, is not a comprehensive environmental regime.

It might be argued that the institutional arrangements adopted at the United Nations Conference on the Human Environment in Stockholm in 1972, which center on the United Nations Environment Programme (UNEP), constitutes a global environmental regime that fits into category VI. The United Nations Conference on Environment and Development in Rio de Janeiro in 1992 sought to develop this regime further. Alternatively, UNEP may be more appropriately viewed as an overarching institutional framework that encourages and facilitates the creation of regimes having a narrower focus.

The final two type regime alternatives, VII and VIII, have a mandate that includes not only the environment, but also other matters pertaining to the use of the domain managed by the regime. The Antarctic treaty system, especially during the 1960s when its membership was still quite small, is an example of a type VII regime in that it deals with military uses of the region in addition to protection of the environment. With the ending of the Cold War, it is possible that a comprehensive regional regime among the Arctic states could be created which would parallel the Antarctic regime.

The regime established by the 1967 Outer Space Treaty, which is open to all states regardless of whether they have active space programs, would be classified as a type VIII regime. Another example is the ocean regime defined by the 1982 Convention on the Law of the Sea. Both are multiple-function regimes that not only address environmental issues, but also establish conditions for a broad range of other uses of these domains.

Proposals have occasionally been advanced for a general Law of the Atmosphere that would be the functional equivalent of the Law of the Sea that would be a comprehensive global management scheme for regulating air pollution and weather modification projects. Such a regime would provide an overarching framework for addressing acid rain, ozone depletion, and global warming, as well as Arctic haze and other more specific atmospheric problems. To the extent that atmospheric problems are intrinsically environmental in nature, such a regime would be a category VI type. If other types of issues – whatever they might be is difficult to envision now – should arise and be addressed by the regime, the appropriate classification would be type VIII.

Regimes having so much breadth have been effective in addressing some issues. However, specific problems, such as Arctic haze, may not have a high enough priority among the members to receive prompt attention.

5. The Status of Regime Development

Of the eight regime alternatives that could provide an institutional framework for mitigating the Arctic haze problem, only two are at some stage of development. The first is the Long-Range Transboundary Air Pollution (LRTAP) regime, established under the auspices of the United Nations Economic Commission for Europe (ECE), which is a type IV regime. It addresses a general category of air pollution and is interregional in involving the states of eastern and western Europe and North America, including all of the Arctic rim states. The second is a nascent type V regime embodied in the Arctic Environment Protection Strategy, which is the product of a diplomatic effort known as the "Rovaniemi process" that began among the Arctic rim states in 1989.

5.1 The LRTAP Regime

As was noted above, the LRTAP regime is an outgrowth of the 1975 Helsinki Accord of 1975, a major East-West agreement that called for cooperation in sectors such as economics, science and technology, and the environment, with transboundary air pollution being mentioned as a specific possibility for cooperation. Soviet General-Secretary Leonid Brezhnev was persistent in calling for a high level meeting on air pollution, which was eventually convened in Geneva by the ECE in 1979 (Jackson 1990). The ECE was chosen for the talks because its membership included the states from both the eastern and western blocs.

The framework treaty on LRTAP that was adopted at the Geneva meetings provides for cooperation on research and reductions of the air pollutants that cause acid rain. A supplemental protocol adopted in 1985 requires a 30 percent reduction of sulphur emissions or transboundary fluxes from 1980 levels by 1993; a 1988 protocol limits nitrogen oxide emissions to 1987 levels by 1994; and a 1991 protocol mandates a 30 percent reduction of emissions of volatile organic compounds (VOCs) from 1988 levels by 1999. Another key part of the LRTAP regime is the Co-operative Program for Monitoring and Evaluation of the Long-Range Transmission of Air Pollutants in Europe, known as EMEP, which includes nearly 100 stations throughout Europe that report to synthesizing stations in Oslo and Moscow.

The members of the ECE established the components of the LRTAP regime primarily in response to the mounting evidence that acid rain was reeking havoc on aquatic life, forests, and cities of the European continent, the southern parts of Scandinavia, and eastern North America. The growing body of scientific knowledge about Arctic haze was not a significant factor in the negotiations on either the framework convention or the protocols (Wetstone 1987).

Nevertheless, the LRTAP regime may already be contributing to a limiting or even lessening of the haze problem. Reductions in sulphur emissions or their transboundary fluxes should diminish the formation of sulphates, which are the principal component of both haze and acid deposition. VOCs, which are to be limited by the latest protocol, are also present in the haze and toxic to fragile fauna and flora of the Arctic region.

Furthermore, the roster of parties to the framework convention not only includes all of the Arctic rim states, but also all of the countries that have been identified as sources of the pollution causing the haze. There are, however, significant holdouts on the protocols, such as Poland, the United Kingdom, and United States in the case of the sulphur protocol.

The LRTAP regime, as it is currently constituted, is not fully suited for addressing the Arctic haze problem. EMEP's data on air quality and deposition of pollutants in the Arctic region is not adequate to support studies on the impact of pollutants on the fragile ecosystems that exist there. Nor does the LRTAP regime address all of the problematic pollutants, such as graphitic carbon, which may impact on the atmospheric radiation balance and albedo of snow and ice, and various heavy metals that are toxic to the species of the Arctic region.

Finally, the value of the 1985 sulphur protocol as a haze reducing instrument is significantly lessened by the clause which permits states to reduce transboundary fluxes as an alternative to limiting emissions generally. It allows Russia to escape any obligation to reduce emissions within its territory that drift across its northern coast out over the Arctic sea, which is one of the principal paths of the haze causing pollutants.

These limitations of the LRTAP regime which diminish its capacity to address the Arctic haze problem could be remedied if the political will exists to expand and strengthen its existing regulations and programs. Given its geographical scope and its mission of regulating transboundary pollution generally, the LRTAP regime is, in certain key respects, the logical institutional framework for addressing the haze problem.

5.2 The Rovaniemi Process

In the aftermath of Gorbachev's Murmansk speech on Arctic cooperation, there has been a flowering of diplomatic activity on the issue of the Arctic environment. The first intergovernmental meeting of the Arctic rim states – namely Canada, Denmark, Finland, Iceland, Norway, Sweden, the United States, and the Soviet Union – was held in Rovaniemi in Finnish Lapland in 1989 (Archer 1990). The group considered, but did not adopt, a Finnish proposal for a framework convention on the northern polar environment that would be followed by protocols on such subjects as transboundary marine and air pollution, wildlife, and radioactive wastes (MacKenzie 1989a and 1989b). Further meetings were held in Yellowknife in the Canadian Northwest Territories in April 1990 and in Kiruna, Sweden, in January 1991.

This diplomatic effort came to fruition with the adoption of the Arctic Environment Protection Strategy at a ministerial meeting in Rovaniemi in June

1991. The Strategy addresses the full gamut of known environmental problems affecting the Arctic region, including the potential damaging impact of air pollutants originating in the mid-latitudes. It recognizes the need for international action to keep air pollutants below critical levels, taking into account the fragility of the Arctic environment. The strategy also calls for an Arctic Monitoring and Assessment Program (AMAP) that, among other things, would observe air quality and deposition of pollutants.

The recent creation of the non-governmental International Arctic Science Committee (IASC) along the lines of the Scientific Committee on Antarctica (SCAR) further enhances the prospects for an effective Arctic environmental regime. The committee was founded at a conference in Resolute, Canada, in August 1990, following a series of meetings dating back to 1986. Potential projects include an inventory of major Arctic scientific activities, a plan for increasing the comparability and compatibility of Arctic data, social scientific research on the inhabitants of the Arctic region, and an Arctic Climate Research Program (Nikitina 1989, p. 128; Østreng 1989, p. 104).

The Arctic environmental regime that grew out of the Rovaniemi process is only in the initial stages of development. It remains to be seen whether it will receive sufficient support from the participating governments to go beyond scientific monitoring and research on the Arctic environment to the more challenging phase of adopting international regulations that minimize disruptive human impacts on the ecosystems of the region. The nascent regime has little potential for mitigating the Arctic haze phenomenon unless the process engages states from outside the region that are largely responsible for haze-forming pollutants.

6. Conclusions

If a choice had to be made between the two existing regimes considered in the preceding section, it appears that the LRTAP regime provides the more promising institutional framework for addressing the haze problem. Its network of research and policy bodies involve all of the countries that contribute to the brew of atmospheric pollutants that form Arctic haze. The regulatory functions of the LRTAP regime already mandate an across-the-board reduction of some of the haze causing pollutants.

With an expansion of the EMEP network in the Arctic region, broader and deeper reductions in emissions of air pollutants, and elimination of the loop hole on transboundary fluxes going over the Arctic ocean, the LRTAP regime could become an effective mechanism for mitigating the Arctic haze problem. The haze problem may be reduced further by the increasingly strict regulations on air pollution being adopted by the European Community and by the self-imposed reductions on emissions of pollutants such as SO_2 and NO_x announced by a growing number of European countries.

As originally constituted, the Arctic Environment Protection Strategy cannot effectively solve the haze problem because the principal polluting states are not among the parties. Furthermore, many years may pass before the Strategy matures into a regulatory regime that can adopt rules or limits on activities that are damaging the Arctic environment. Nor is there any assurance that the haze problem will be one of the top priorities for regulatory action in view of the regime's broad mandate to preserve the Arctic environment.

These two regimes should not, however, be looked upon as mutually exclusive or wastefully redundant alternatives for addressing Arctic haze. Rather they could become complementary regimes, which together may be the most effective arrangement for international cooperation on the haze problem. The monitoring and research programs of the Arctic regime, in particular the newly created Arctic Monitoring and Assessment Program (AMAP), may be coordinated with the LRTAP's EMEP program. This information base, when combined with the findings of the research programs of the non-governmental International Arctic Science Committee, could buttress scientific knowledge on the magnitude and consequences of transboundary air pollution over the Arctic to the point that the parties to the LRTAP regime would give a higher priority to mitigating the Arctic haze problem.

Notes

1. For periodic overviews of scientific knowledge on Arctic haze, see Rahn and Heidam (1981); Barrie (1986); and Barrie et al. (forthcoming).
2. The Network convened subsequent conferences at the University of Rhode Island (1980), in Toronto (1984), in Hurdal, Norway (1987), and in Copenhagen (1991). Papers from the Rhode Island, Toronto, and Hurdal conferences are published in special issues of the journal *Arctic Environment* (1981, 1985, 1989). The Scott Polar Research Institute in Cambridge, England, hosted another major symposium on Arctic air pollution in 1985 (see Stonehouse 1986).

References

Archer, Clive, 1990. 'Arctic Cooperation: A Nordic Model', *Bulletin of Peace Proposals*, Vol. 21, No. 2, pp. 165-74.
Atmospheric Environment, 1981. 'Arctic Symposium II', Vol. 15, No. 8.
Atmospheric Environment, 1985. 'Arctic Symposium III', Vol. 19, No. 12.
Atmospheric Environment, 1989. Special Issue on 'Arctic Air Chemistry', Vol. 23, No. 11.

Barrie, Leonard A., 1986. 'Arctic Air Pollution: An Overview of Current Knowledge', *Atmospheric Environment*, Vol. 20, No. 4, pp. 643-63.

Barrie, Leonard A., Olson, M. P. and Oikawa, K. K., 1989. 'The Flux of Anthropogenic Sulphur into the Arctic from Mid-latitudes in 1979/80', *Atmospheric Environment*, Vol. 23, No. 11, pp. 2505-12.

Barrie, Leonard A., Gregor, D., Hargrave, B., Lake, R., Muir, D., Shearer, R., Tracey, B. and Bidleman, T. (forthcoming). 'Arctic Contaminants: Sources, Occurrence and Pathways', in *Science of the Total Environment*.

Benedict, Richard, 1991. *Ozone Diplomacy: New Directions in Safeguarding the Planet*. Cambridge: Harvard University Press.

Carey, John, 1988. 'Peering into the Mystery of Arctic Haze', *International Wildlife*, Vol. 18, No. 2 (March-April), pp. 27-8.

Haas, Peter M., 1990. *Saving the Mediterranean: The Politics of International Environmental Cooperation*. New York: Columbia University Press.

Heintzenberg, Jost, Hansson, Hans-Christen, Ogren, John A. and Odh., Sven-Ake, 1985. 'Concept and Realization of a Air Pollution Monitoring Station in the European Arctic', *Ambio*, Vol. 14, No. 3, pp. 150-5.

Jackson, C. Ian, 1990. 'A Tenth Anniversary Review of the ECE Convention on Long-Range Transboundary Air Pollution', *International Environmental Affairs*, Vol. 2, No. 3 (Summer), pp. 217-26.

MacKenzie, Debora, 1989a. 'Environmental Issues Surface at the Summit of the World', *New Scientist*, No. 1653 (February 25), p. 29.

MacKenzie, Debora, 1989b. 'Arctic Protection Awaits American Involvement', *New Scientist*, No. 1688 (October 29), p. 28.

Maxwell, J. Barrie and Barrie, Leonard A., 1989. 'Atmospheric and Climatic Change in the Arctic and Antarctic', *Ambio*, Vol. 8, No. 1 (March 16), pp. 42-9.

Mitchell, J. Murray, Jr., 1957. 'Visual Range in the Polar Regions with Particular Reference to the Alaskan Arctic', *Journal of Atmospheric and Terrestrial Physics*. Special Supplement, pp. 195-211.

National Research Council, 1979. *Airborne Particles*. Baltimore: University Park Press.

Nikitina, Elena N., 1989. 'International Mechanisms and Arctic Environmental Research', *Current Research on Peace and Violence*, Vol. 12, No. 3, pp. 123-32.

Osherenko, Gail and Young, Oran R., 1989. *The Age of the Arctic: Hot Conflicts and Cold Realities*. Cambridge: Cambridge University Press.

Østreng, Willy, 1989. 'Polar Science and Politics: Close Twins or Opposite Poles in International Cooperation', in Steinar Andresen and Willy Østreng (eds.), *International Resource Management: the Role of Science and Politics*. London: Belhaven Press, pp. 88-113.

Ottar, B., 1989. 'Arctic Air Pollution: A Norwegian Perspective', *Arctic Environment*, Vol. 23, No. 11, pp. 2349-56.

Rahn, Kenneth A., 1979. 'Arctic Haze Provides a Clue to Polar Circulation', *Maritimes*, Vol. 23, No. 1 (February), pp. 8-11.

Rahn, Kenneth A., 1984. 'Who's Polluting the Arctic', *Natural History*, Vol. 93, No. 5, pp. 30-8.

Rahn, Kenneth A. and Heidam, N. Z., 1981. 'Progress on Artic Air Chemistry, 1977-1980: a Comparison of the First and Second Symposia'. *Atmospheric Environment*, Vol. 15, No. 8, pp. 1345-48.

Rahn, Kenneth A. and Shaw, Glenn E., 1982. 'Sources and Transport of Arctic Pollution Aerosol: A Chronicle of Six Years of ONR Research', *Naval Research Reviews*, Vol. 24, pp. 3-25.

Roginko, Alexei Yu., 1989. 'Arctic Environmental Cooperation: Prospects and Possibilities', *Current Research on Peace and Violence*, Vol. 12, No. 3, pp. 133-43.

Stonehouse, B., 1986. *Arctic Air Pollution*. Cambridge: Cambridge University Press.

United Nations Conference on the Human Environment, 1972. *Report of the United Nations Conference on the Human Environment*. UN Doc. A/Conf. 48/14.

United Nations Environment Programme, 1989. *Register of International Treaties and Other Agreements in the Field of the Environment*. UNEP/GC.15/Inf. 2.

Wetstone, Gregory S., 1987. 'A History of the Acid Rain Issue', pp. 163-95, in Harvey Brooks and Chester L. Cooper (eds.), *Science for Public Policy*. New York: Pergamon Press.

6 Sustainable security: an Inuit perspective

Dalee Sambo

1. Introduction

The concept of "sustainable security" is a relatively new concept to most governments and people. However for indigenous peoples it is a concept and way of life that was successful until the coming of Europeans to the Americas. From the time of contact forward, indigenous peoples have found themselves struggling to regain the sustainable security they once knew and by which they lived.

This chapter will focus on the Arctic and will address, from an Inuit perspective, the concept of sustainable security, before contact, the gradual deterioration of indigenous security, and finally, it will introduce a prescription of elements that would allow indigenous peoples to achieve sustainable security in a rapidly changing world.

2. Before Contact

Recently I was listening to my great Aunt telling stories of her childhood along the coast of the Norton Sound in western Alaska. I was struck by the repeated statements she made about her lack of fear and sense of security in this beautiful and wild setting. "We were never of afraid of anything". She was really talking about the contrast that she has seen in her lifetime. She feels that there is much to fear today. Her sense of security has been altered by the social change that has taken place around her.

The natural order of things has changed. The natural order is now threatened and a different order has been replaced for what was once an order dictated by the natural environment and the peoples' relationship to it.

The Inuit of the circumpolar zone are a hunter/gatherer culture that relied primarily upon the ocean's riches for sustenance. Because of their dependence upon the ocean and lands they were highly nomadic, travelling from region to region, or making other long distance excursions.

The Inuit were organized communally, practicing a "primitive form of socialism" (Morgan 1947) like many other indigenous cultures. In all matters, the collectivity was more important than the individual. Leaders were chosen based upon their ability to hunt and provide for the community as a whole. A balance also existed between women and men because the combined skills of women and men were needed for survival.

The village sites were selected for a number of reasons: safety and shield from unpredictable and often turbulent weather, availability of fish and other marine mammals, and opportunity to build shelter. In short, the challenges facing the Native peoples before contact were generally limited to shelter, food, weather and other environmental factors.

The only threats to the security of these indigenous cultures were the possible crashes in species population which caused starvation and death or the threat of a neighboring tribe or nation encroaching upon tribal hunting grounds. These natural fluctuations or warring between indigenous cultures were the only times that insecurity entered into the lives of indigenous communities.

From the point of first contact with outsiders to the present time, indigenous peoples have suffered immensely. This is where the transformation and change of the natural order begins, and too often, has ended in devastation of Native cultures and peoples.

3. Contact and Demise of the Indigenous Concept of Security

It is not a coincidence that indigenous societies in the North and elsewhere are in a state of deterioration. Along with the deterioration of indigenous societies comes the deeply felt insecurity. Unfortunately, the indigenous perspective of contact reads like a horror story for most, if not all, indigenous peoples. The intent to convert indigenous peoples and bring them under the "sovereignty" of kings, queens and other foreign powers created widespread strife despite some of the early attempts to ensure "friendly treatment" of the Natives. The maltreatment, enslavement, suicide, punishment for resistance, malnutrition due to destruction of natural environment or over-exploitation of natural resources, and introduction of disease for which indigenous peoples had no natural immunity have all taken its toll on the indigenous populations in the North. One example of dramatic population decline occurred during the first two generations of Russian domination from 1762 to 1800 in the Aleutian Chain area where there was a population decline of 80 to 90 percent (Damas 1984).

Along with population decline came the destruction of the traditional social order. There was a desire on the part of the European invaders throughout the North to deal with only one "permanent authority". Hence the village leaders were no longer the best hunters, but an authority figure identified and defined by the outsiders. Change also took place in the economic order with the introduction of cash and the notion that things could be bought and sold. This added the stress of a new economic environment quite opposite from the traditional economic order of most indigenous communities. These were all alien concepts to the collective social organization of the Native communities. The creation of new conditions and problems for social order, control and security put most indigenous communities out of balance. Since first contact, these conditions have only been compounded by the political and legal forces of the western world.

The legacy of outside control is what indigenous peoples today are fighting against. Since the time of first contact there has always been strong resistance to change. Certainly some adaptation has taken place over the last 500 years. However, there remains a desire to identify oneself and community as indigenous. The desire persists to regain a strong sense of security in the face of rapid social change.

4. Human Rights Violations

In the *Alaska Native Claims Settlement Act* of 1971 Congress abolished the aboriginal rights of Alaska Natives, including their aboriginal rights of hunting, fishing and trapping. Congress had spoken. Yet twenty years later Alaska Natives refuse to acknowledge the loss of their tribal right, their right as collectivities, to take fish and wildlife and to regulate their own subsistence activities (Berger 1991).

It makes a kind of sense to us: here the great landowners and their military protectors, here the middle class, there the urban reformers, in the bush the guerillas, many lives at risk. All of this we can comprehend. But we cannot comprehend the wholesale destruction of Indian villages, the murder of tens of thousands of Indians carried out for no apparent reason (Berger 1991).

In the North and in every sector of the globe, indigenous peoples and nations are still impeded in every conceivable way from proceeding in peace with their own development. States are apprehensive of the rights that exist, so they choose to deny the existence of indigenous peoples or deny indigenous rights (International Work Group on Indigenous Affairs Yearbook 1990). There are hardly any regions of the world where the territorial rights and other fundamental rights of indigenous peoples are not seriously and repeatedly ignored, devalued or otherwise violated by governments.

Presently there is no legal framework that fully recognizes indigenous rights within an indigenous context.[1] The all-important collective dimension of indigenous rights must be at the core of such a legal framework. Without explicit and proper protection of collective indigenous rights, distinct societies and cultures would remain unnecessarily exposed to deterioration from outside forces, and in some cases, destruction.

Indigenous peoples and nations continue to suffer atrocities and abuses that are or should readily be condemnable human rights violations. Yet existing international human rights instruments do not satisfactorily accommodate the fundamental human rights of indigenous peoples. In the absence of appropriate international standards, indigenous peoples are too often the main targets or victims. In addition, they are the last to be accorded fair consideration.[2]

In regard to indigenous peoples, human rights related issues that are persistently ignored or denied include self-determination, land and resource rights, development, peace, participation in matters that directly and indirectly affect indigenous communities, recognition as distinct societies, hunting and fishing rights, and environmental security ... just to name a few (Hannum 1990). This is generally the case worldwide and certainly prevalent in many places in the Arctic. The lack of adequate respect for fundamental human rights is a major contributing factor towards greater insecurity and instability in indigenous communities.

5. Environmental Threats

The profound relationship that Native peoples have to the environment is a matter that cannot be sufficiently underscored. Indigenous peoples of the Arctic have been anxiously attempting to fend off the threats of environmental destruction. In the North, environmental warning bells have been going off since the time of first contact. As "inhospitable" as the Arctic may seem to outsiders, it still is not safe from the rest of humankind.

5.1 Oil and Gas Development

In light of milder temperatures, improved infrastructure and accessibility, scientific research and oil and gas development activities have been underway in the Arctic for some time. The Trans-Alaska Pipeline System (TAPS) and offshore oil development in the Beaufort and Chukchi Seas have caused great alarm about the adverse impacts of oil and gas development in the Arctic. Long-held fears were unfortunately confirmed by the recent Exxon Valdez oil spill. This major oil spill, in relatively mild northern waters, should be seen as a forewarning of future catastrophe in the colder waters of the Arctic Ocean.

Unfortunately, the estimates of oil in the North are high and this has fueled the search for oil (Kindt & Parriott 1984; Mast et al. 1989). Research shows potential in both on-shore and off-shore areas of Alaska, Canada, Greenland, Norway, and Russia.

Recently Gulf Canada Resources Limited revealed its worst case scenario for an oil blow-out in the Beaufort Sea. The result would be a spill nearly ten times the size of the one created when the Exxon Valdez ran aground off Alaska. The company estimates that an uncontrolled well could spill 40,000 barrels of oil a day into the environmentally sensitive Beaufort Sea for at least 60 days, while a relief well was being drilled to kill the blow-out (Globe and Mail, April 10, 1990, p. A1). It is important to note that this is an industry estimate and not some *worst case scenario* prepared by an over-enthusiastic environmental organization. The oil industry itself is admitting the potential for serious and devastating impacts on the off-shore Arctic environment by oil development.

5.2 Ozone Layer Depletion and Air Pollution

More and more evidence is being published about the impacts of global environmental problems in the high latitudes of the Arctic. The United Nations Environment Program (UNEP) estimates that the ozone layer over the Arctic is deteriorating at the rate of 3 percent annually (see Doolittle 1989; Brunee 1988). Among the many adverse effects of stratospheric ozone layer depletion is the damage to shallow-dwelling marine organisms, which are an essential part of the overall food chain. In 1986 an Arctic hole was discovered. No depletion was observed in 1987 or 1988, but the hole reappeared in 1989 (Roots 1990).

Despite accurate information, global warming or the accumulation of *greenhouse gases* may be affecting the Arctic permafrost temperatures. Boreholes in Alaskan permafrost show that the surface temperature in that area has warmed as much as 4 degrees centigrade in the past century and that the warming is apparently continuing (Roots 1990). Global warming could have devastating effects in the Arctic and elsewhere through weather changes and flooding of low-lying areas (Smith 1978).

Pollution sources in or affecting the Arctic are many and varied. For example, there are highly industrialized locations like the Kola Peninsula and White Sea region of northwestern Russia, and the large metallurgical complexes of north-central Siberia.[3]

The prevailing winds carry air-borne pollutants over the central Arctic Basin and the rivers deliver their contaminants to the Arctic Ocean. The rapid transport of the radioactive contaminants from Chernobyl in southwestern Russia to northern Scandinavia is a recent unfortunate demonstration of deposit of toxic atmospheric pollution in the Arctic. Arctic haze, now common, in the springtime, consists of soot, hydrocarbons, and sulfates. In addition, the northwest Atlantic currents and ice conditions help to deliver chemically stable or slow-reacting pollutants from industrialized eastern North America.[4]

Evidence of the presence of toxic pollutants like cadmium, mercury, and polychlorinated biphenyls (PCB's) entering the Arctic food chains have resulted in a higher level of identifiable chemicals (used only in the south) in Inuit who have eaten the seals, whales and other mammals. Studies have shown the presence of PCB's and other organochlorine contaminants in body tissue and mothers' milk.[5] All of these forms of pollution raise atmospheric, biological and human health issues.

5.3 Ocean Dumping

Ocean dumping, including the intentional disposal of radioactive waste at sea is another major threat. Though the London Dumping Convention (LDC) from 1972 includes sixty-three nations as contracting parties, the mere existence of the Convention does not prevent dumping operations. All eleven of the Arctic nations are parties to the LDC, yet it has been asserted by environmental organizations that Canada and the United States are members of the "dumpers club" and randomly dump toxic materials and waste into the ocean.

Recently an ocean dumping officer of Environment Canada stated "our fees are a joke, really they are. If you've got 10,000 cubic meters of toxic materials, we charge $1,000. In a land waste-disposal site, you would probably pay close to a million." The same article provided the following information: there have been approvals for and dumping of 5.7 million cubic meters of dredging materials; 686,000 cubic meters of construction rubble; 151,580 cubic meters of fish offal; 2,000 tons of garbage from ships; 20,000 cubic meters of fish-pickling brine; 10,000 tons of wallboard; and 200 firearms seized by police (Bueckert 1990). This is just for 1989 and the ocean dumping program in Canada has been going on for fifteen years.

What are the policies and practices of the other Arctic states, as well as the non-Arctic states who traverse Arctic waters? Some wastes are toxic, like the dredged material taken from industrial areas, contaminated with heavy metals, synthetic chemicals, oil and grease.[6] It is also worth noting that the LDC provides a military exception or exception for vessels that enjoy sovereign immunity with regard to pollution from ships.[7]

5.4 Militarization

One cannot discuss Arctic environmental threats without speaking of militarization. The presence of nuclear-powered ballistic missile submarines, bombers, long-range cruise missiles, air launched cruise missiles, all pose potentially devastating effects on Arctic peoples and the environment. Examples include widespread radioactive pollution, as a result of accidents involving aircraft carrying nuclear weapons or marine vessels that are nuclear-powered or nuclear-armed and testing of weapons in the Arctic. These concerns are not unfounded: recall the radioactive accident of the US B-52 bomber crash near Thule, Greenland, in 1968, when four hydrogen bombs were on board (Peterson 1988).

The total number of nuclear disasters at sea is unknown to the general public. There are currently 15,000-16,000 naval nuclear weapons worldwide (Arkin & Handler 1989) and these nuclear weapons are routinely present on all US and Russian aircraft carriers, logistics support ships, submarines, and most surface warships that are able to carry them. The most recent (April 7, 1989) accident occurred when the Russian Mike-class submarine, a nuclear powered attack vessel carrying two nuclear torpedoes, sank in the Norwegian Sea (Arkin & Handler 1989).

From 1945 to 1989, 50 nuclear weapons and 11 nuclear reactors have been lost at sea. In this same period there were 212 confirmed accidents worldwide involving nuclear-powered vessels (Arkin & Handler 1989). Three years ago the USS Nimitz visited the Port of Anchorage, Alaska, and the public swarmed to see the ship. Little did they know that this same vessel, in May 1979, had a primary coolant leak. Further, the Soviet icebreaker "Lenin" is known to have had the most serious reactor accident. The US Navy reported that "there is strong evidence that this ship experienced a nuclear-related casualty in the 1960's requiring the ship to be abandoned for over a year before work was begun to ultimately replace [its] three reactors with two" (Arkin & Handler 1989). Although it remains uncertain, it is likely that this vessel originally embarked from the Port of Murmansk (the Russians most active ice-free port) on the coast of the Kola Peninsula.

Scientists have also argued that although technology has advanced, the accidents continue. The escalation of military activity in the Arctic, generally combined with the history of nuclear-related accidents, make the threats to the Arctic "theater" very real in nature.

Low-level test flights in Labrador and Quebec have been on-going for years in Canada's North. The Innu of Labrador and Quebec/Nitassinan, have been calling for a ban of such test flights for years. Such flights have numerous adverse environmental, social, cultural, health, and Innu security effects (Tennant & Turpel 1991). The proposal for a NATO base at Goose Bay, Labrador, has been canceled, however, low-level test flights will continue due to a previous agreement. According to *Ploughshares Monitor*, June 1990, currently there are about 9,000 flights per year and these flights could grow to as many as 18,000 per year under the existing training agreement with Germany, the United Kingdom, the Netherlands, and the United States.

The recent break-up of the Soviet republics and the uncertainty of the future military regime in the former Soviet Union does not generate any security, either here in Alaska or anywhere on the globe. Without a logical arms control or arms reduction initiative in response to the collapse of the once centrally-controlled military, real security in the North will remain elusive.

5.5 Environmental Security

The global community now has a better understanding and assessment of the level of damage done by the Gulf War. There is general consensus about the damage and destruction caused by this unfortunate conflict. The costs include: the thousands of human lives lost, oil spills that have had devastating effects on turtles, marine mammals and migratory birds, the oil fires and the black rain that has fallen.

Saddam Hussein's direct, intentional and wanton use of environmental destruction as a *tool of war* should alarm people everywhere. At the same time, the indirect environmental destruction caused by the *Coalition forces* should not be underestimated. The connection between this environmental destruction and armed conflict has prompted many to consider the concept of *environmental* or *ecological security*.[8]

The world community is becoming acutely aware of the fact that states can no longer exercise sovereignty or assure their own security in isolation from one another. Environmental problems like those addressed above, many of which are global, do not recognize the artificial boundaries that states have established primarily through aggression. Dependence upon renewable and non-renewable resources themselves can create conflicts that states have never properly considered. It has been suggested that a major motivating factor for US involvement in the Gulf War was to guarantee future access to oil, a non-renewable natural resource.

Another example is the diminishing supplies of fresh water. Those in need may turn to armed conflict to satisfy their demands. In response to the proposal by Ethiopia to damn the headwaters of the Blue Nile, Egypt's President Anwar Sadat said in 1978: "We depend upon the Nile 100 percent in our life, so if anyone, at any moment, thinks to deprive us of our life we shall never hesitate [to go to war] because it is a matter of life or death" (Gleick 1991).

For indigenous peoples, the call for environmental protection has been used as a tool to combat government and industry in their pursuit of profits. Too often the only result has been the destruction of not only the traditional environment of indigenous peoples but indigenous communities as well.

One case in point is that of the James Bay II hydro-electric project in Northern Quebec, presently under debate in Quebec and Canada. Phase I of this megaproject (La Grande) prompted the so-called settlement of Cree and Inuit claims but at the same time it has left a significant portion of Cree traditional territories flooded and a traditional way of life in disarray. They must now fight back in the courts of law and of world public opinion. Discovery of oil in Alaska prompted a similar response, but there the Exxon Valdez oil spill has destroyed the subsistence economies of the Natives of Prince William Sound. Development, in the name of economic security, has too often created great inequities and unsustainable development.

The profound relationship that indigenous peoples have with the environment, which includes social, economic, cultural and spiritual dimensions, must not be overlooked in the present discussion on environmental security and *sustainable security*. For cultures that have flourished as an integral part of the ecosystem, the environmental disruption cannot continue to be weathered by them. Their dependence upon the environment remains highly significant.

6. The Fight to Regain Sustainable Security — International Legal Developments

The layers that subjugate indigenous cultures are many and varied. They include the lack of recognition or respect of their distinct cultures and fundamental human rights; bureaucracies and industries reflecting only non-indigenous economic values and interests in the North; inadequate or unjust land agreements; policies of assimilation or termination; social and cultural programs dictated by external forces; and denial of political rights and political participation.

Modern international law and national legal orders around the world have subsumed the rights of indigenous peoples and nations.[9] These legal orders are extremely Eurocentric and they have been largely successful in the subordination of collective indigenous rights to self-determination, lands and resources, and subsistence. In total, destructive to the sustainable security once enjoyed by indigenous peoples.

However, much has been done by indigenous peoples themselves to reverse this continuing trend of marginalization and exclusion. The recent history of indigenous rights at the international level has been very positive.[10] Indigenous peoples are increasingly taking steps to ensure that they have the opportunity, at the international level, to speak out about their common issues and fundamental concerns, and the need for international attention to further protect, preserve and promote their unique status and rights. These international indigenous human rights standard-setting processes should be seen as a significant tool that indigenous peoples can use to re-build or re-store sustainable security in their homelands.

Indeed, through these processes, the international community is being encouraged to provide for the evolution of indigenous rights within a positive law framework. Indigenous peoples are slowly returning as an international personality within the international legal order. This evolution can also be viewed as the exercise of their right to development: political development.

The various political and legal rights that must be accorded proper recognition within the framework of states will take time and effort to satisfactorily achieve their full accommodation. For some Northern indigenous peoples, certain rights have been recognized and an appropriate regime implemented. This is particularly true in Greenland through the development of the Home Rule Government by Inuit. Sometimes rights are dealt with in an unsatisfactory fashion, like the case of the Alaska Native Claims Settlement Act of 1971. The Alaska Native Claims Settlement Act of 1971 dealt with land rights only and did not address the matter of self-determination or political rights. Furthermore, the United States Congress unilaterally 'extinguished' certain rights in an ambiguous fashion. In other cases, there still exists a need to affirm rights and negotiate suitable arrangements. For example, in Canada, an important and potentially far-reaching constitutional debate on self-government is taking place at the national level.

International standard-setting processes are beginning to devise minimal legal standards which states must adhere to, in order to ensure the continued survival and development of indigenous peoples. Such processes are increasingly taking place with the participation of indigenous peoples in relevant national and international initiatives. It is absolutely critical that the international community and states include indigenous peoples in policy- and decision-making. Such indigenous involvement must be both substantial and continuous. Relations of state governments with indigenous peoples must be fully consistent with the principle of equal rights and self-determination of peoples. These relations must be based on principles of cooperation and respect, rather than on unilateral state action.

The "Brundtland Report" (1987) addressed the need for respect for indigenous land and resource rights as well as involvement in matters that directly affect their lands and ways of life. This report and its widespread adoption by decision-makers has strengthened the case for participation by indigenous peoples. The Report also gave recognition to the unique situation of indigenous peoples:

> The starting point for a just and humane policy for such groups is the recognition and protection of their traditional rights to land and other resources that sustain their way of life, rights they may define in terms that do not fit into standard legal systems. These groups' own institutions to regulate rights and obligations are crucial for maintaining harmony with nature and the environmental awareness characteristic of the traditional way of life. *Hence the recognition of traditional rights must go hand in hand with measures to protect the local institutions that enforce responsibility in resource use. And this recognition must also give local communities a decisive voice in the decisions about resource use in their area* (Brundtland Report 1987).

In response to mounting pressure from indigenous groups, the United Nations Economic and Social Council established the Working Group on Indigenous Peoples (WGIP) in 1982. The WGIP mandate is to review conditions of indigenous peoples and to draft a Universal Declaration on Indigenous Rights. The WGIP meets annually to conduct its work. The most recent draft of the WGIP Declaration is fairly far-reaching.[11] However, additional work must be completed in order to respond to the aspirations of indigenous peoples. The ongoing resistance of government representatives will have to be effectively confronted. The WGIP hopes to finalize the draft this year and forward it to the Sub-Commission on Prevention of Discrimination and Protection of Minorities, the Commission on Human Rights, the Economic and Social Council and to seek final approval of a text by the United Nations General Assembly in 1993.

In addition, the Organization of American States has embarked upon the drafting of an international legal instrument elaborating upon the rights of indigenous peoples in the Americas. To date, they have drafted a document entitled *The Status and Rights of the Indigenous Peoples of America*. They have also circulated to governments and non-governmental organizations, a questionnaire on the rights that should be contained in such a Convention or Declaration. The World Bank, succumbing to pressure by concerned organizations and indigenous peoples, has prepared an *Operational Directive*, September 1991, on Indigenous Peoples. Though this latter document is not far-reaching enough, it is a substantive first step towards the recognition of indigenous rights when it comes to the future development activities of the World Bank.

To date, the only legally binding international instrument that substantiates and reinforces indigenous rights is the recently revised International Labor Organization's *Indigenous and Tribal Peoples Convention* (No. 169), now open for state ratification. The out-dated ILO Convention No. 107 remains in force for 27 different states worldwide.[12] It is important to note that these are merely minimum international standards and are not norms that are considered adequate by indigenous peoples or the ILO itself. During the 1990 and 1991 sessions of the UN Working Group on Indigenous Peoples, the ILO commented that the Working Group and the UN generally should surpass the ILO standards contained in Convention 169. However, there are certain important protections that this Convention provides:

- guaranteed respect for the "integrity" of indigenous peoples and their rights (Article 2, para. 1)
- protection of indigenous cultures and environment (Article 4, para. 1)
- in order to protect and preserve the environment of indigenous territories, state governments must take measures in cooperation with the peoples concerned (Article 7, para. 4 and Article 33)
- cooperation should include the planning, coordination, execution and evaluation stages of any such measures proposed (Article 33, para. 2a)
- respect for indigenous values, practices and institutions (Articles 2, 3 and 5a and b)
- indigenous rights to decide their own priorities and process of development as it affects their lives, beliefs, institutions, spiritual well-being and lands (Article 7, para. 1)
- right to participate in the formulation, implementation, and evaluation of plans and programs for national and regional development which may affect them directly (Article 7, para. 1).

These are just some of the examples of the international standards that have been developed and which should be regarded as minimum standards that states must respect and recognize.

Specific initiatives have been undertaken by a number of indigenous non-governmental organizations. One key example is the Inuit Circumpolar Conference (ICC).[13] The ICC initiatives include the pursuit of an Arctic zone of peace; establishment of an International Arctic Council; participation in the International Arctic Science Committee (IASC) and the so-called "Finnish Initiative"; active membership in the International Union for Conservation of Nature and Natural Resources and involvement in IUCN's establishment of an Inter-Commission on Indigenous Peoples; and participation in a full range of militarization issues in the Arctic. In addition, the ICC has gained Russian Inuit participation within the framework of the ICC and they have also furthered collaboration with other Arctic indigenous peoples, including the Sami, through the Arctic Leaders Summit.

7. Conclusion

Given the history of indigenous peoples and their rights and the deterioration of sustainable security, as well as the more recent developments related to the struggle to return to a level of security in indigenous communities, the strategies and methods to achieve sustainable security are becoming more clear to indigenous peoples and others around them.

The author has chosen to outline the environmental threats in a detailed fashion to demonstrate the lack of sustainable security that exists in the North, not only for Arctic-rim countries but even more so for the indigenous peoples, the first peoples of the Arctic. There is a need to deal with sustainable security in comprehensive terms. We must not only understand the relationship between war, environmental degradation and development but more importantly, we should be strengthening and elaborating upon the relationship between peace, human rights and development.

The prescription of elements needed to generate greater security include: initiatives based on the principle of self-determination; full respect for land and resource rights; recognition of the right to development and the right to peace; direct participation in international, national and regional processes that affect indigenous communities and peoples; respect and recognition of indigenous values; recognition as distinct societies; security in hunting and fishing rights; the right to a safe and healthy environment; and removal of the threat of environmental destruction.

All of these elements, if fully recognized and respected, could eliminate the state of insecurity that indigenous peoples live in today. Significant progress is being made. However, more must be done with a renewed sense of urgency.

The degree of deterioration of indigenous communities is still a "measuring stick" for sustainable security. Are indigenous communities now regaining their strength and vitality? If they are restoring their health, they can make an important contribution to worldwide security. Not enough has been done to involve indigenous peoples directly in decision- and policy-making. Indigenous peoples must be involved through consensual arrangements with other governments. This alone would generate greater security. In most conflicts, indigenous values are not respected. There still remains a constant imposition from outside, with little or no recognition of indigenous self-determination.

Respect for values, recognition of rights, and basic equity are reliable paths towards achieving sustainable security in a genuine and permanent sense. Without them, indigenous communities will continue to be marginalized. If all of these elements could be woven together in a manner that is consistent with the perspectives and aspirations of each indigenous nation, indigenous peoples could achieve a sustainable security that would benefit not only their own communities and territories, but also the world community.

Notes

1. The only existing international legal instrument specifically addressing indigenous rights is International Labor Organization *Convention 169 on Indigenous and Tribal Peoples*, 1989. However, it must be stated that Convention 169 contains many shortcomings with respect to the fundamental human rights of indigenous peoples. In particular, the ILO does not have the "competence" to deal with the political rights of indigenous peoples and is strictly limited to social, cultural and economic rights.
2. Examples of unilateral state actions include the 1988 Canada/United States Agreement on Arctic Cooperation and the 1989 Canada/USSR Agreements on Arctic Cooperation (Mulroney-Gorbachev Summit in Moscow, November 1989).
3. See 'Report of the Meeting', Protecting the Arctic Environment, Yellowknife Preparatory Meeting, April 18-23, 1990, Report of Working Group I on the State of the Environment, where Arctic pollution problems include acidification, chlorinated organics, oil, radioactivity, heavy metals and noise.
4. See above.
5. See 'State of the Arctic Environment Report on Chlorinated Organics', Technical Background Paper, Draft Report for the Finnish Initiative Meeting, Indian and Northern Affairs Canada, April 1990.
6. For a further discussion on the dumping of dredged materials, see generally, 'Ocean Dumping: Progress Towards a Rational Policy of Dredged Waste Disposal', *Environmental Law Reporter*, Vol. 12, 1982.

7. Article 8, para. 4, Convention on the Prevention of Marine Pollution by Dumping of Wastes and Other Matter, done at Washington, London, Mexico City, and Moscow, December 29, 1972. Entered into force for the United States, August 30, 1975; and also Article 3, Section 3, International Convention for the Prevention of Pollution from Ships, done at London on November 2, 1973.
8. See Conclusions of the 'Conference of Experts on the Use of the Environment as a Tool of Conventional Warfare', Ottawa, July 2-12, 1991, convened by the Government of Canada and the Secretary General of the United Nations. See also P. Gleick, 1991. 'Environment and Security: The Clear Connections', *The Bulletin of the Atomic Scientists*, April 1991; D. Deudney, 1991. 'Environment and Security: Muddled Thinking', *The Bulletin of the Atomic Scientists*, April 1991; P. Mische, 1990. 'Ecological Security in an Interdependent World', *The Ploughshares Monitor*, Vol. XI, No. 4; 1989. 'Environmental Security', *The Ploughshares Monitor*, 1989.
9. See generally S. J. Anaya, 1990. 'The Capacity of International Law to Advance Ethnic or Nationality Rights Claims', 1990 Conference of the USSR-USA Scholars' Dialogue on Human Rights and the Future.
10. For a more thorough historical review of indigenous rights at the international level, see S. J. Anaya, 1990. 'The Right of Indigenous Peoples and International Law in Historical and Contemporary Perspective', *Harvard Indian Law Symposium*. For general discussion of the international indigenous human rights developments see R. Barsh, 1986. 'Indigenous Peoples: An Emerging Object of International Law', *American Journal of International Law*, Vol. 80; Muntarbhorn, 'Realizing Indigenous Social Rights' and Daes, 'On the Relations Between Indigenous Peoples and States', *Without Prejudice*, Vol. II, No. 2, 1989.
11. Preambular and Draft Operative Paragraphs to the Draft Declaration as Submitted by the Members of the Working Group. UN Documents E/CN.4/Sub.2/AC.4/1991/CRP.1; CRP.2 and CRP.4.
12. The International Labor Organization (ILO) has two conventions in place for the protection of indigenous rights: ILO Convention No. 107 (1957), currently in force; and Convention 169 (1989), open for ratification.
13. The Inuit Circumpolar Conference (ICC) was organized in 1977 in Barrow, Alaska, under the direction of its founder, the late Mayor Eben Hopson of the North Slope Borough. Since 1983, the ICC has held non-governmental organization status with ECOSOC. Presently they represent Inuit throughout Alaska, Canada, Greenland and the Russian Far East. They can be contacted directly at: ICC Head Office, 650 32nd Avenue, Suite 404, Lachine, Quebec H8T 3K4, Canada.

References

Arkin, Wm. and Handler, J., 1989. 'Nuclear Disasters at Sea, Then and Now', *Bulletin of the Atomic Scientists*, July/August.

Berger, T. R., 1991. *A Long and Terrible Shadow*. Vancouver/Toronto: Douglas & MacIntyre.

'Brundtland Report', 1987. *Our Common Future*. London: Oxford University Press.

Brunee, 1988. *Acid Rain and Ozone Layer Depletion: International Law and Regulation*. New York: Transnational Publishers.

Bueckert, D., 1990. 'Tonnes and Tonnes of Garbage Dumped Annually in Oceans Off Canada', *Gazette*.

Damas, D. (ed.), 1984. *Handbook of North American Indians*. Washington, D.C.: Smithsonian Institute.

Doolittle, M., 1989. 'Underestimating Ozone Depletion: The Meandering Road to the Montreal Protocol and Beyond', *Ecology Law Quarterly*, Vol. 16.

Gleick, P., 1991. 'Environment and Security: The Clear Connections', *The Bulletin of the Atomic Scientists*, April 1991.

Globe and Mail, April 10, 1990, p. A1.

Hannum, H., 1990. *Autonomy, Sovereignty, and Self-Determination. The Accommodation of Conflicting Rights*. Philadelphia: University of Pennsylvania Press.

International Work Group on Indigenous Affairs Yearbook. 1990.

Kindt, J. and Parriott, T., 1984. 'Ice Covered Areas: The Competing Interests of Conservation and Resource Exploitation', *San Diego Law Review*, Vol. 21.

Mast, R. F. and others, 1989. 'Estimates of Undiscovered Conventional Oil and Gas Resources in the United States - A Part of the Nation's Energy Endowment'. Washington, D.C.: U.S.G.S.

Morgan, M., 1947. *Bridge to Russia*. New York: E. P. Dutton and Co.

Peterson, N., 1988. 'Denmark, Greenland and Arctic Security', in K. Möttölä (ed.), *The Arctic Challenge: Nordic and Canadian Approaches to Security and Cooperation in an Emerging International Region*. London: Westview Press.

Roots, F., Environment Canada, 'The Arctic Environment and its Role in International Relations', paper for meeting of the Working Group on Arctic International Relations (WGAIR). Moscow/Murmansk, Russia, January 1990.

Smith, B., 1978. 'United States Arctic Policy 2', Center for Oceans Law and Policy.

Tennant and Turpel, 1991. 'A Case Study of Indigenous Peoples: Genocide, Technocide and Self-Determination', *Nordic Journal of International Law*.

7 The role of Sami traditions in sustainable development

Elina Helander

1. Introduction

The Sami people are an ethnic minority who are indigenous to Finland, Sweden, Norway and Russia. Most of them inhabit areas north of the Arctic Circle, but in Norway and Sweden the Sami area extends southwards to around the 62nd parallel.

The Sami population is today estimated at about 50,000 to 70,000, the vast majority (between 40,000 and 45,000) living in Norway. The greatest concentration of Samis is found in the province of Finnmark, where they number about 25,000. The Sami people were originally fishermen and hunters, but they have since adopted other livelihoods such as reindeer herding and farming. Today, Sami people are engaged in most occupations of modern society.

In Norway, less than 10 % of the Sami people are reindeer herders. In Sweden, where the total Sami population is estimated at around 17,000, some 2,700 are involved in the reindeer industry. About half of the Swedish Samis live in the traditional Sami regions. The Finnish Sami population numbers approx. 5,700, of whom 3,800 live in the Sami territory. Half of the Finnish Samis are involved in the reindeer business. Estimates from Russia are that the Sami population there numbers about 2,000, many of whom live in the Lovozero region on the Kola Peninsula. Traditionally their most important sources of income are reindeer breeding and fishing, but recently there has been a growing movement of Russian Samis into larger towns.

68 Elina Helander

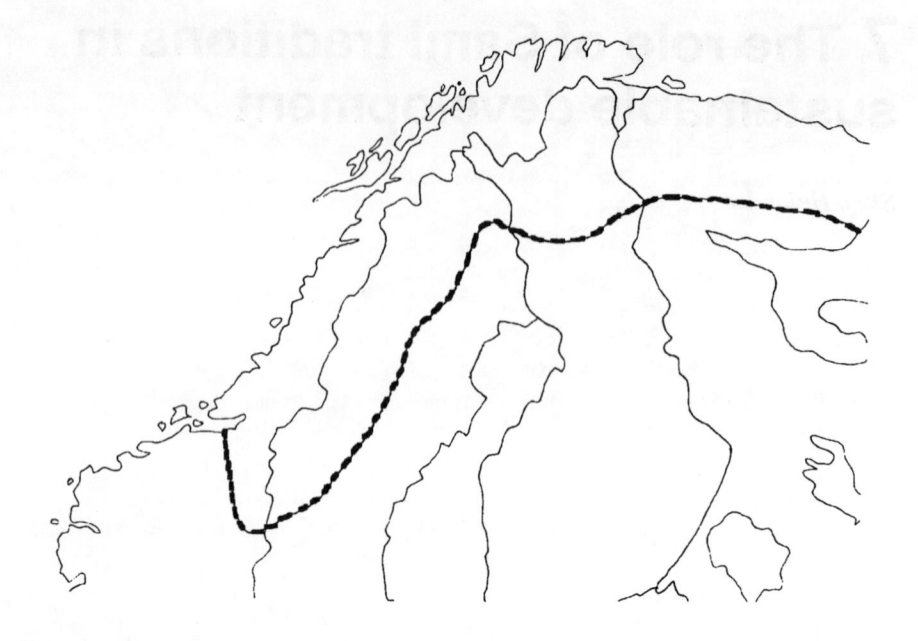

Figure 7.1 General map of the Sami areas in Norway, Finland, Sweden and Russia

There are three different dialects in the Sami language: East Sami, Central Sami and South Sami. Two thirds of the Sami population speak some form of Sami.

The Sami people and their political organizations have a coordinating body in the Nordic Sami Council, which was established in Karasjok in 1956. A democratically elected body called the Sami Assembly or *Samithing* has recently been set up in Norway. Sweden and Russia have no similar bodies to represent the Sami people. The founding of the Nordic Sami Institute in Kautokeino in 1973 provided an important impetus for Sami research into the needs and values of Sami society (see also *3.4* below).

2. The Dynamics of Tradition

It is not easy today to venture out on an objective discussion on the meaning of tradition in modern society; the risk is that one is immediately denounced as a conservative reactionary or romantic who wants to go back to the times of manual labouring and backward economic order. None the less there are widespread fears that the pace of change in modern society represents a serious threat to tradition, especially where the identity of an ethnic minority is closely linked up with tradition.

2.1 Tradition as an Active Process

Tradition may be defined as consisting in those cultural elements that are handed down from one generation to another (Honko 1981, p. 16). It may derive from past times and from distant locations, and it can be adapted to the actual shape of a culture. Tradition lends continuity to culture, but in order to do this it must be constantly reproduced.

As well as a host of active traditions, every culture has a reserve of more or less idle traditions that are not in continuous or habitual use. Among these traditions one will often find elements that run counter to the mainstream values in the society concerned. It is important to note that tradition is fundamentally an active process; traditions that are in everyday use are in a constant state of flux, shaped by an endless succession of choices and new priorities.

All this means that the preservation of tradition is not a goal in itself in any given culture; it is important to remain free from all mechanical preconceptions of the preservation of tradition (Honko 1981, p. 56). Instead, one must concentrate on the dynamics of tradition and on the role of tradition in providing an ethnic group with its identity, its distinctive life-style, economic system, etc. Researchers have also been showing a growing interest in synchronic situations where traditions live and procreate rather than looking simply at the growth and development of individual traditions.

2.2 The Continuity of Ethnic Models

The concept of 'tradition' is closely bound up with those of 'culture' and 'ethnicity'. Here, tradition is defined and understood as the matter out of which culture is formed. A common assumption in research is that ethnic identity is intimately intertwined with certain core elements in a given culture (Ruong 1981; Smolicz 1981). Although certain cultural characteristics still constitute an important criterion for the ethnic identity of the Sami people, these features are hardly applicable to all Samis in modern society.

One of the key strategies adopted by the Sami people in their own struggle for cultural survival has been to clearly define their identity. An important milestone was the 7th Nordic Sami Conference in Gällivare, Sweden, in 1971, where the following statements were laid down in a Sami political programme (cf. 1980, p. 2):

    1. We, the Samis, are one people and the borders of nations shall not divide the community of our people.

    2. We have our own history, our own traditions, our own culture and language. We have inherited the rights to land and water from our

forefathers and our right to conduct our own forms of trade.
3. It is our inalienable right to manage and develop our forms of industry and communities according to our common terms and we, together, will manage our lands, natural resources and national heritage for coming generations.

In general it seems that the issue of cultural survival under the pressure of accelerating social change has attracted increasing attention in the recent academic debate. The evidence suggests that ethnic groups can indeed maintain their integrity and identity in spite of those pressures. Ethnicity is regarded as a legitimate basis for enduring social relationships and political mobilization (cf. Williams 1979). Modernization and centralization have tended to increase ethnic activities.

Some researchers seriously suspect whether traditional life-styles and ethnic models:

> can work any more in a world that has seen several centuries of global communication and fairly violent culture contact. And this may be all the good, for regional ethnicity can easily turn into a provincial type of ethnic chauvinism, which finally results in a *narrowing* of human possibilities (Berman 1988, pp. 297-8).

The importance of traditional life-styles is given due attention in the Brundtland Report, which points out that these can teach modern society many important lessons (Vår gemensamma framtid 1989, p. 26).

3. What is Knowledge?

Theoretical definitions of the concept of knowledge abound. In the discussion below the aim is to abstract from these a reasonably coherent definition that will serve the purposes of the analyses that follow.

3.1 Definitions

My baseline assumption is that knowledge exists. Further, I assume that there are three types of knowledge: 1. scientific knowledge, 2. practical knowledge and 3. implicit knowledge.

The continuing growth of scientific knowledge is widely regarded as the main problem of the theory of knowledge. Scientific knowledge aims to be clear, objective, impartial and comprehensive. Without going into a detailed discussion of the scientific method, suffice it to observe that this, at least within Western culture, has long been regarded as the only relevant way of gathering and accumulating knowledge.

As regards practical and implicit knowledge, the former is based on practice and skills while the latter involves culturally inherent understanding. Implicit knowledge is a sort of background knowledge, an instinctive familiarity with the underlying premises of action and thought which is difficult to either define or challenge (see also Helander 1991).

3.2 Traditional Knowledge Systems

Traditional knowledge systems are defined as the patterned ways in which people from a non-literate tradition learn about their reality and communicate such information amongst themselves and from generation to generation (Waldram 1986, p. 116; see also Freeman 1988). According to this understanding, tradition-based knowledge is comparable to scientific knowledge because it has the same structure as science. Traditional knowledge is based on observations that span across a long period of history. It has the concepts that are needed to describe knowing, and it is also involved in the process of verification.

Some thinkers such as Capra and Sorokin are convinced that the paradigm in Western society is now changing. Sorokin says that Western culture is not only going through a crisis but it is in fact in a state of transition. According to Sorokin, the knowledge system which the Western world now knows is '*sensate*'. The world is viewed from a materialistic and mechanical standpoint. Values are short-lived, knowledge is fragmented, and reason is employed instead of intuition (cf. Lindholm 1985).

Capra (1989, p. 15) has a very similar line of argumentation:

> what we need, to prepare ourselves for the great transition we are about to enter, is a deep re-examination of the main premises and values of our culture, a rejection of those conceptual models that have outlived their usefulness, and a new recognition of some of the values discarded in previous periods of our cultural history.

He continues (1989, pp. 24-5):

> it is now becoming apparent that over-emphasis on the scientific method and on rational, analytic thinking has led to attitudes that are profoundly anti-ecological /.../ Ecological awareness, then, will arise only when we combine our rational knowledge with our intuition for non-linear nature of our environment.

3.3 The Sami Concept of the Environment

There is no doubt in my mind that traditional knowledge has a major part to play in the efforts to resolve the ongoing global crisis as well as in the further, sustainable development of modern economies.

The traditional Sami livelihoods have always sought to live in harmony with the environment, to avoid upsetting the delicate balance of nature. This is achieved through a system of self-regulation in that if one sector of production or one particular resource fails to yield, then there is always another source to fall back on until such time as the first one has recovered.

The Sami concept of the environment consists of several different components, including the natural environment, the cultural environment, the social environment and the linguistic environment. These elements go together to make up a whole which must always be viewed as one single entity. If one of the elements changes, there will necessarily be changes in the other elements as well (cf. Sara 1978).

According to the Sami Programme for the Environment (1990, pp. 19-20), the environment in the Samiland:

> is very sensitive and can easily be subjected to wear and damage which cannot be repaired for centuries, if ever. Our society is being subjected to constant influence which is transforming our pattern of life and our relationship with nature. /.../ Piece by piece, other nations have taken our land and our water from us. Their relationship to nature is bidding fair to impoverish the environment of Sápmi. /.../ We are part of the ecosystem. Our cultural manifestations are adapted to an ecological balance between what nature can give and what we can utilize in relation to nature's productive capacity. /.../ Ours is a living culture, always enabling us to adapt to various natural conditions, acquiring new knowledge which will enable us to survive. /.../ Our language expresses the way in which we perceive the environment. At the same time it is a necessary vehicle for the transmission of knowledge from one generation to another. /.../ Language has an important part to play in expressing our responsibility for maintaining the ecological balance in nature. /.../ The social environment can easily respond to changes both in the natural environment and in the various cultural elements.

3.4 The Nordic Sami Institute

The first research institute specializing in Sami issues — the Nordic Sami Institute — was established in Kautokeino, Norway, in the early 1970s. Here, Sami researchers work on their own terms, applying methods and concentrating on problems that are directly applicable to Sami society.

4. Reindeer Herding

Reindeer herding is not only a Sami industry; it is a whole way of life. Having said that, the primary concern today is more and more with meat production.

Reindeer meat accounts for 1 % of total meat production in Norway; in 1985 production of reindeer meat amounted to 2,000 tons. Less than 10 % of the 40,000 Sami people in Norway earn their living from reindeer herding.

The industry today has become increasingly capital-intensive; the number of herders is generally decreasing (with some local exceptions such as Kautokeino) and the size of herds is increasing. Traditionally, reindeer herders have flexibly combined this job with fishing, hunting, berrypicking, etc. in order to guarantee a sufficient income.

4.1 Traditional Organizational Units

The traditional organizational units of Sami reindeer herders are the '*siida*' and the '*báiki*' (family). The *siida* is a unit through which common reindeer-herding tasks are organized. The *báiki*, then, is an independent unit which can be included in different *siida*. Tasks at the *siida* level are concerned with the reindeer herd as a single unit and at the *báiki* level with individual animals as private property.

In the management of reindeer, it is a realistic goal for the individual to become a reindeer keeper in conjunction with a family-based *báiki*. Those who have only a few animals may be engaged in other production activities as well. Compared with hunting and fishing, for instance, reindeers are thought to be a far more dependable source of income in the long term. However, even in reindeer herding profits may vary from year to year.

Reindeer herders build their dwellings in relation to the *báiki*, i.e. according to the annual cycle of migration. These dwellings are built for purposes of handling and servicing certain products and equipment and for exchanging information. Traditionally, a *báiki* represented a unit which had all the necessary skills to manage the herd and which at the same time served as the primary source of information and socialization.

The number of *siidas* varies during the year depending on operational considerations; in this sense the *siida* is a highly flexible organization. The land of a *siida* has traditionally been 'owned' by a given family.

It is through this organization that each individual wins his or her social function and worth. Each person belongs first to a *báiki*, which in turn forms part of a *siida*. By way of general understanding on a *siida*'s traditional link to an area, a geographical basis is created for its production operations.

4.2 The Formal Organization of Reindeer Production

Reindeer herding is regulated and protected by legislation. The Reindeer Herding Act of 1978 stipulates within the Sami reindeer territory in Norway that reindeer may only be herded by a Sami whose parents or grandparents have been herders.

The control function lies with the relevant government bodies which may decline permission to set up new enterprises. A central concept here is the '*operational unit*', as defined in the Reindeer Herding Act, which implies that a reindeer herd is owned and managed by an accountable leader. A ceiling may also be set for the number of operational units in a given area.

Today, there are some 250,000 reindeer in the whole country. In the Kautokeino area, comprising some 25,000 km^2, the number is around 100,000 reindeer, which in 1988 were owned and managed by 290 leaders for operational units. The total number of people engaged in reindeer herding is of course much higher. In Finnmark, 50 % of the reindeer herders are aged between 30-50 years. The vast majority or 90 % are men (see NIBR-rapport 1990).

Since 1977 the Sami Reindeer Herders' Association in Norway has negotiated a special reindeer herding agreement with the national government. Reindeer herding has thus become a government-regulated economic activity on a par with farming and fishing. The Reindeer Herding Act specifies the areas of the relevant counties that are to be regarded as reindeer grazing areas. These are the regions of reindeer herding: East Finnmark, West Finnmark, Troms, Nordland, North Trøndelag, South Trøndelag/Hedmark, which are further divided into districts.

Local reindeer herders have official representation through district boards, which are annually elected for each herding district from amongst the reindeer herders. The relevant county councils appoint a regional board for each grazing area for a period of four years. The regional boards come under the administration of the National Reindeer Herding Board. One of the main tasks of the regional boards is to regulate the size of reindeer herds and the number of herd units in the districts.

The National Reindeer Herding Board is appointed by the Ministry of Agriculture from amongst nominees proposed by the NRL (Sami Reindeer Herders' Association) and other appropriate associations. The National Reindeer Herding Board acts in an advisory capacity to central government authorities. At the top of the hierarchy is the national government. The Directorate of Reindeer Herding was established in 1979, and it is answerable to the Ministry of Agriculture. Its main task is to supervise and monitor the implementation of the objectives of the Reindeer Herding Act and the reindeer agreement (see The Sami People 1990, pp. 172-80).

4.3 Changes in Reindeer Management

Recent years have seen many important changes in the management of reindeer herding. These are the result of various developments:

> 1. With the continuing growth and expansion of modern technology, reindeer herding has increasingly become a matter of meat production. The day-to-day herding job requires less people than before, but they must have the strength and stamina and technical competence that is required by work with skidoos, off-road vehicles and other modern equipment. The vehicles

cause serious damage to the pasture. There is less work now for women, children and old people, and there is an obvious risk that people who have extensive traditional knowledge and an ecological approach to their job will no longer be needed in reindeer management. Communication, the outflow of information and socialization in concrete situations have all weakened. Language-based knowledge (place names, expressions, ecological terminology, etc.) is growing thinner. The increasing use of technology may eventually even disintegrate the unity of *báiki*.

2. The increasing popularity of permanent housing means that families are becoming cut off from their reindeer herds, and they no longer take part in the spring and autumn migrations. Permanent housing also increases costs, which in turn means that families need to increase their incomes; consequently, women are moving out of the family business into wage employment. In earlier years and decades children learned the skills of the trade on the job, whereas today they spend more and more time at school rather than in traditional working units. Child-raising at home is now increasingly left to the women.

3. The school institution is unable to provide training and education in traditional skills. Modern education in reindeer herding tends to alienate young people from reindeer keeping. The reindeer herding society encourages 'informal education' in daily work.

4. The above factors have made it increasingly difficult to train young people in reindeer management.

5. The administrative system that is based on non-Sami traditions and values tends to create disorder.

6. Reindeer herding areas have been shrinking in size and deteriorating in quality because of the growth of industry, increasing pollution and the construction of new power plants, public roads, airports, etc.

7. In some cases the formal division of reindeer grazing areas is in conflict with the traditional *siida*-based concepts. The problems are worse on common lands because the number of animals exceeds the grazing resources. To take advantage of the situation, the individual reindeer herder is tempted to increase the size of his herd, which obviously serves to intensify the competition for limited resources. The problem is known as the tragedy of the commons.

5. Samiland — a Periphery

5.1 Decision-making

As we saw earlier, one of the cornerstones of the Sami identity is the principle of solidarity which says that the Sami are one people who are not divided but united by the national borders that run between them. Conscious efforts are now under way to develop a uniform policy and ideology that applies to all Sami people on all sides of the national borders.

None the less the fact remains that the Sami people live in four different countries and therefore live under different systems of public administration, which in turn means that they are affected by different political decisions. The countries concerned have somewhat different policies on minorities, even though there are some attempts at harmonization now.

In all countries political power is exercised by the central government, and even quite recently we have seen decisions made in Oslo and other capitals that have directly affected the Sami people but that have been made without even listening to local opinion. A good example is provided by the decision of the Norwegian government to open the grouse hunting season in mid-September, against the Sami proposal that it should start two weeks late. Other similar decisions have been made with regard to fishing, duck-shooting, limitations on skidooing, etc.

Ideological power, then, lies in the hands of the school institution and the mass media. Sami schools and the Sami media are still fairly undeveloped today and their ideological function remains limited, but it is none the less on the increase.

In Norway the affairs of the Sami people are governed by the Sami Assembly, which started work in 1990 after the first democratic elections in September 1989. The debate on the Sami Assembly, which will be seeking to take a leading role in the future political development of the Sami situation in Norway, has so far concentrated on the status and authority of this body. The Assembly's administrative functions are restricted to granting funds to certain Sami organizations and bodies in accordance with guidelines issued by the Ministry. The long-term goal is to increase the powers of the Sami Assembly, but for the time being it has merely an advisory position. Recently there have been calls to the effect that the Sami Assembly should be given decision-making authority over the use of land, an issue which is of crucial importance to the survival of the people (Lasko 1991, p. 116).

5.2 Cultural Division of Labour

Most Sami people live in Arctic regions, which means that have had to develop a culture that can help them survive in a cold climate. I have in mind, most particularly, the people's ecological know-how, their extensive expertise on resource management and land-use. However, this expertise remains very much unexploited both in the practical planning and in the legislation of Sami commerce. There is a cultural division of labour that governs the life of the Sami people; the decision-making authority, more often than not, lies with administrative bodies consisting of non-Sami members.

According to a recent study by the Nordic Sami Institute, the Sami people are also heavily underrepresented in the decentralized tertiary industries at all levels of skills. Also, Sami farmers have received a far smaller share of the capital and subsidies invested in farming than non-Sami farmers living in the same area. The same applies to the fishing industry (Gjerde & Mosli 1985, pp. 53-60; see also The Sami People 1990, p. 113).

5.3 Natural Resources

Almost all of the land traditionally inhabited by the Sami people is owned by the state; for example, in the province of Finnmark in northern Norway, the state owns about 90 % of the land. In the Sami region and particularly in northern Norway, there are vast natural resources such as fish, crude oil and gas that are all exploited by outsiders, i.e. southern or foreign companies. The Sami people have no say in setting the price of these commodities, nor do they get any share of the profits.

One of the key strategies to resolve the employment problem in the north is tourism, but again the problem remains that a large part of the profits are pocketed by companies from the south.

5.4 Environmental Threats

In the homeland of Russian Samis on the Kola Peninsula, a different problem is developing with the widespread destruction of the area's natural resources. Already this has affected the environment in the Sami reindeer breeding areas on the Norwegian side of the border. In addition, nuclear tests have been carried out in northern Russia for several decades. The effects of Chernobyl are also felt in this region, for they have been far more widespread than was first implied, reaching well beyond the immediate radius of the accident (cf. Heininen 1990).

6. Sustainable Development

The ongoing debate on the issue of sustainable development originates from the observation that the present trends in economic and environmental development in the world are not sustainable. The concept was coined in the BrundtlandReport of 1987, which defined sustainable development as an effort to satisfy present needs without jeopardizing the possibilities of future generations to satisfy their needs (Vår gemensamma framtid 1989, p. 22). The Brundtland Report takes a broad perspective on the issue and looks at it from a social, economic, cultural and ecological point of view, also discussing such questions as poverty and the situation of women.

However, the concept of 'development' is not necessarily fully compatible with the notion of 'sustainable'. The important thing to bear in mind is that 'development' is not a spontaneous movement but always the result of intentional activity within a given society. Also, the term can be and has been used to cover up negative developments or effects such as pollution.

It seems that it is impossible to have a universal model of sustainable development that could be applied to the whole world. Instead, we need to stress the importance of local control, local actions and local solutions (see Pretes & Robinson 1989). What and how are we going to sustain? What are we going to develop and how? It is clear that the concept of sustainable development needs to be further elaborated and that more research is needed.

7. From Periphery to Centre

The following measures are suggested for a sustainable development from the point of view of the Sami people:
- Sami areas must be recognized as having an independent value of their own rather than being regarded simply as a source of raw materials for outside actors;
- the Sami political organs must be given responsibility and control over the area's natural resources;
- all planning and decision-making that affects the Sami people must be based on Sami participation;
- the knowledge of the Sami people as well as their social and economic systems must be respected;
- the natural resources in the Sami area must not be destroyed;
- Sami researchers must be given more resources to do their work;
- economic life should be based on more local activities, local labour and local decision-making;
- the Sami concept of the environment must be respected.

References

Berman, M., 1988. *The reenchantment of the world.* New York: Cornell University Press.
Capra, F., 1989. *The Turning Point Science, Society and the Rising Culture.* Glasgow: William Collins Sons & Co. Ltd.
Freeman, M. M. R., 1988. 'Ethnoscience, prevailing science and Arctic co-operation'. *Paper prepared for International Conference on Arctic Co-*

operation. Toronto. 26-28.10.1988.

Gjerde, A. and Mosli, J. H., 1985. *Samiske næringers plass i samfunnsplanlegginga.* Dieðut 1985, No. 5. Kautokeino: Sámi Instituhtta.

Habermas, J., 1988. *Kommunikativt handlande. Texter om språk, rationalitet och samhälle.* Uddevalla: Daidalos.

Hechter, M., 1976. 'Group Formation and the Cultural Division of Labour', *American Journal of Sociology,* Vol. 84.

Heininen, L., 1990. 'An introduction', in L. Heininen (ed.), *Arctic Environmental Problems.* Occasional Papers No. 41. Tampere Peace Research Institute.

Helander, E., 1991. 'Samiska traditioner, traditionell kunskap och bärkraftig utveckling'. Soon to be published in, *Nord-Nytt. Nordisk tidsskrift for folkelivsforskning.*

Honko, L., 1981. 'Traditionsekologi - en introduktion', in L. Honko and O. Löfgren (eds.), *Tradition och miljö. Ett kulturekologiskt perspektiv.* Lund: LiberLäromedel.

Lasko, L.N., 1991. 'Självbestämmanderätt', in *Samernas 14. konferens.* Lakselv 4-6.8.1989. Ohcejohka: Sámiráðði.

Lindholm, S., 1985. *Kunskap. Från fragment till helhetssyn.* Stockholm: LiberFörlag.

Lov om reindrift av 09.07.78, Nr. 49 med ändringar senast 21.12.84.

NIBR-rapport, 1990, No. 11. *Mot et bærekraftig samfunn i Indre Finnmark. Reindriftsøkonomi og ressursgrunnlag i en samfunnsmessig sammenheng.* Norsk Institutt for by- og regionforskning.

Pretes, M. and Robinson, M., 1989. 'Beyond boom and bust: a strategy for sustainable development in the North', in *Polar Record,* Vol. 25, No. 153.

Ruong, I., 1981. 'Samerna. Identitet och identitetskriterier', in Nordnytt. *Nordisk tidsskrift for folkelivsforskning,* Vol. 11.

Samepolitiskt program, 1980. Ohcejohka: Sámiráðði.

Sara, A. N., 1978. 'Grunnprinsipper i urbefolkningens politikk', in *Kultur på karrig jord. Festskrift til Asbjørn Nesheim.* Oslo.

Sara, M. N., 1990. *Badjeealáhusláhki ja boazodoallopolitihkka.* Dieðut 2. Guovdageaidnu: Sámi Instituhtta.

Smolicz, J., 1981. 'Core values and cultural identity', in *Ethnic and Racial Studies,* Vol. 4, No. 1.

The Sami Programme for the Environment, 1991. Ohcejohka: Sámiráðði.

The Sami People, 1990. Karasjok: Sámi Instituhtta & Davvi Media O.S.

Vår gemensamma framtid, 1989. Rapport från Världskommissionen för miljö och utveckling. Stockholm: Prisma/Tiden.

Waldram, J. B., 1986. 'Traditional knowledge systems: the recognition of Indigenous history and science', in *Saskatchewan Indian Federated College Journal,* Vol. 2, No. 2.

Williams, C. H., 1979. 'Ethnic resurgence in the periphery', in *AREA,* Vol. 11, No. 4. Institute of British Geographers.

8 Knowledge-based development in the North: new approaches to sustainable development

J. D. House

1. Introduction

The northern regions of the global economy, including northern Canada, the United States (Alaska), Scandinavia and the Soviet Union present unique problems for the advocates of sustainable development. Their fragile environments make a strategy of heavy industrialization particularly troublesome, as can be seen dramatically in the ecological devastation of the Kola Peninsula. Nevertheless, northern populations of natives (Inuit, Innu and Sami) and non-natives (whites who have settled in the north) aspire for a better standard of living and a better quality of life; and decision-makers in the south view the exploitation of northern resources as a new frontier for increasing national wealth.

How can the needs of the environment and the needs of people be reconciled in the northern peripheries of advanced industrial countries? There is no simple answer. But we can make a start at least by shifting the focus from industrialization and resource-based development to *knowledge-based development* in the periphery. We need first to understand the systemic pressures for industrialization and naked resource exploitation, and then take action to counteract these pressures, which threaten ecological degradation, through an alternative approach to sustainable development compatible with a post-industrial age.

2. World Systems Theory and Its Limitations

World systems theory provides a powerful tool for analysis, as can be seen in the chapter by W. L. Goldfrank in this collection. There are indeed inexorable forces at work in industrial economies, in both private and state capitalist forms, which tend to extend the logic of industrial expansionism the exploitation of natural resources and the growth of heavy industry wherever located to all corners of the globe, from Brazilian rain forests to Arctic islands. Karl Polanyi (1944) was ahead of his time in pointing out that the ultimate logic of a market society is the destruction of land (the environment) and labour (people). This insight applies not just to a market society, but to any industrial society that takes the *mastery* of nature as its guiding principle.

No society in history pursued this principle as ruthlessly as the Soviet Union. In the Soviet north west, the devastating effects of untrammelled industrial growth and resource exploitation demonstrate dramatically how this logic can destroy the natural environment and thereby, if left unchecked, the foundation of life itself.

World systems theory is indeed a powerful tool for analysis, but it goes astray when it falls into the temptation of mistaking systemic *tendencies* for *inevitabilities*. This is equally the case for the optimistic historicism of Marxism as it is for the domesday prognostications of many modern environmentalists. For to show that the evolution of a particular socio-economic system is heading in a certain direction is *not* to show that it must inevitably reach its destination. It can be stopped along the way, or diverted into a different direction through human agency. People make their own history.

This can be seen in the twentieth century history of socialist principles in different societies. With the wisdom of hindsight, the Soviet Union can be seen as a tragic experiment: an attempt to implement in practice the historicist predictions of Marxism. In the Scandinavian social democracies, by contrast, human agency intervened to counteract many of the worst tendencies of unbridled industrial capitalism. The Finnish consensus model of industrial relations, for example, is a successful mechanism for preventing the extreme class polarization predicted by Marx.

In a similar vein, human agency must intervene to counteract the late twentieth century tendency of industrial expansionism to wreak ecological havoc. From the perspective of a social actionist critical social science, world system's analyses of destructive socio-economic tendencies is simply the first step toward taking action to prevent those tendencies from becoming actualities.

In the present context, the challenge is to adopt a strategic approach to economic development in the north which would *not* harm the natural environment. This is the meaning of sustainable development. *Knowledge-based development* is such an approach. The case of Labrador will be used to illustrate the argument.

3. Labrador

Labrador is the northern and mainland part of the Province of Newfoundland and Labrador is located off Canada's east coast. In terms of political and economic decision making, Labrador is doubly peripheral. The provincial capital is the city of St. John's, located at the eastern extremity of the Island of Newfoundland far from the towns and villages of Labrador. The Province of Newfoundland and Labrador, in turn, is ruled politically by the federal capital, Ottawa; and the Province is highly dependent on federal transfers and equalization payments to maintain a reasonable standard of living that is nevertheless the lowest of all ten Canadian provinces. The Province is also dependent *economically* on central Canada and the United States. The rich iron ore mines of western Labrador, for example, are owned by central Canadian companies which in turn are owned and controlled by American steel companies.

Labrador is a vast, sparsely populated land mass, with only 28,741 inhabitants in 1986 living in its 265,437.43 square kilometres. Despite its location between 51°15' and 60°30' degrees latitude, the frigid Labrador current which runs along the coast gives the region an Arctic-like climate and vegetation, with long, cold winters and short summers. The culture and way of life is also akin to more northern peoples. The coast of Labrador is dotted by 20 incorporated and 11 unincorporated small communities dependent on an uncertain seasonal fishing industry. Today, most households depend on government transfer payments, especially unemployment insurance (UI), for a significant proportion of their income. The inland town of Happy Valley-Goose Bay contains a military base from which pilots from several NATO countries practice low-level flying.

The population of coastal and central Labrador comprises five distinct groups. About 3,000 Inuit live in the communities of Nain, Makkovik, Hopedale and Happy Valley-Goose Bay; some 1,500 Innu live in the towns of Davis Inlet and Sheshashit; and many "Settlers" of mixed European and native origin are located in several of the communities; many whites from the Island of Newfoundland and elsewhere have more recently made Labrador their home; and there is a continuing turnover of military, government and other personnel from the master institutions of Canadian society.[1]

Western Labrador is very different from the coast. It is constituted by three industrial towns: Labrador City and Wabush are mining towns and Churchill Falls is the headquarters of a large hydroelectric project. Most of the 12,165 residents of western Labrador came originally from the Island of Newfoundland, but many of them have settled and now call Labrador home. The people of Labrador have a distinct identity as Labradorians, and there is much resentment of Newfoundland and the provincial government for not paying enough attention to Labrador and its needs.

The native peoples, the Inuit, Innu and Settlers have their own identities and remnants of their traditional cultures. The Inuit and Settlers, who often cooperate with one another, are trying to work with federal and provincial agencies to further their economic development, while also pursuing land claims for large parts of Labrador. The Innu are also pursuing land claims, but they have adopted an anti-development stance, at least until the land claims issue has been settled. They have demonstrated, with some success, such developments as low-level flying and the construction of a road for building a pulp and paper mill.

4. Knowledge-Based, Sustainable Development for Labrador

The main contention of this article is that a focus on *knowledge-based* rather than *resource-based* development is the key to sustainable development for Labrador and similar northern regions. This section describes the main features of such an approach to knowledge-based, sustainable development. The conclusion addresses the issue of *agency* for social change. What historical agent or agents can be counted on to bring about the kind of progressive change advocated here?

4.1 Features of Knowledge-Based, Sustainable Development

Knowledge About Ecology and Sustainability. Human ecology is an old and well-established viewpoint within social science which contends that the relationship between human beings and their natural environment is *fundamental* to understanding social life.[2] The Brundtland Report gives a non-theoretical, *moral* dimension to this approach. We should, indeed must, pay heed to relationships between humans and their natural environment if we are to survive as a planet.

This knowledge about the relationship between people and their environment is the starting point for knowledge-based sustainable development. The question is: how can we best protect and capitalize on the natural environment so as to achieve sustainable development, that is economic development that at best enhances and is at worst neutral vis-à-vis the integrity of the natural environment? All proposed developments must be examined in light of this question.

A natural implication of this is that the people of Labrador themselves must be made knowledgeable about environmental issues and sustainable development, and so must the authorities in St. John's and Ottawa who make decisions that impact on Labrador. Environmental awareness and environmental education must be integral to both local people's and outside decision-makers' understanding of economic development. We can no longer afford to pigeon-hole environmental concerns in one compartment and economic development concerns in another. Sustainable development demands that decisions be made and monitored by people *knowledgeable* about the link between economic development and the environment.

Appropriate Development, Technology and Organization. Sustainable development is *appropriate* development appropriate to the people, their culture, the land, the sea, and the resources on the land and in the sea. It is development that threatens the integrity of none of these. This in turn requires the use of *appropriate technology*, technology that allows the husbanding of a resource rather than its mastery and ultimate destruction. For example, the use of large factory trawlers using indiscriminate mobile fishing trawls to exploit the stocks of cod and other species off the coast of Labrador is *inappropriate*. In time, it leads to the destruction of the resource itself. The traditional inshore fishery of coastal communities, using small boats and fixed, passive fishing gear is more appropriate. It allows both for the protection of the resource and the sustaining of local communities.

This is not to suggest that appropriate technology is necessarily old-fashioned or archaic. New appropriate technologies need to be designed to lengthen the fishing season, to allow the storage of fish during the *glut* season of high catches for processing later, to ensure a high quality product and to expedite the transportation of the product to world markets. Appropriate technologies both protect the resource base and allow for more efficient local economies that produce greater *gross community products*.

But such a progressive approach to sustainable development is only likely under conditions of *appropriate organization* political, economic and social decision-making arrangements that ensure the primacy of environmental concerns. What is the appropriate organization? Many critics of the current situation have pointed out, rightly, that most major decisions that affect Labrador's development are made outside the region, by corporate capitalists and politicians that, because they are not directly affected, have little concern about the environmental impacts of their decisions. The flooding of the Smallwood reservoir for the massive Upper Churchill hydroelectricity project in western Labrador, which destroyed thousands of acres of natural vegetation and wildlife, is a much cited example.

Unfortunately, however, it would be too simplistic to suggest that the devolution of decision-making to local people would solve the problem. Settlers and whites in Labrador are just as keen on industrial development as are most outside authorities; and native peoples too have been known to destroy resources by poaching and overfishing. While knowledge of local conditions must guide the decision-making process, it is equally important that decision makers at all levels be knowledgeable of their decisions, and that environmental concerns be paramount.

Some progress along these lines has been evident in Labrador in recent years. Both the federal and provincial governments now require that thorough environmental impact assessments be carried out before any major new development projects are approved. The process is not perfect, but it is a great improvement over past practice. The Labrador regional office of Enterprise Newfoundland and Labrador, a new crown agency of the provincial government, gives more decision-making powers to the region and allows for more education of and more input from local people in economic development decision-making. In support for their demands for just land-claims settlements, native peoples in Labrador and neighbouring northern Quebec have been surprisingly effective in stalling such developments as low-level military flying, the growth of a pulp and paper industry in Labrador and the expansion of further large-scale hydroelectric projects.

Mindless industrial expansionism is no longer the taken for granted rule for economic development in Labrador. This is not to suggest by any means that sustainable development has won the day, but it is at least a promising pre-condition for that to occur. Optimistically, Labrador *could* be at a transition stage toward knowledge-based, sustainable northern development. Another necessary pre-condition is that developers adopt a new approach to resource industries.

A New Approach to Resource Industries and Controlled Industrialization. In the new, knowledge-based economy, resource industries will continue to be important, but their development will be *controlled by knowledge* so as to support sustainability. Natural resources, which are nothing more than parts of the environment socially defined as having value, must be seen in the context of the larger ecological system in which people interact with nature. Given that *the first priority for long-term economic development in Labrador is to preserve and enhance the natural environment itself*, the management of natural resources should be ruled by this larger imperative. Natural resources have a role to play but they are not the be-all and end-all of economic development. The development of our natural resources should be *subordinate* to the need of the environment and the needs of people, rather than the reverse which has been the case until recently.

Nevertheless, it must be recognized that the needs of people in Labrador, natives and non-natives alike, include pre-eminently the needs for positive economic growth, enterprise creation and employment generation. Labrador has an official unemployment rate of around 20 per cent. Natural resources will continue to have an important role to play in this; but it should be a controlled role guided by the principles of sound ecology.

What is this role? As we look toward the twenty-first century it is useful to distinguish two categories of resource industries. The first category is *established resource industries*. In Labrador, these are trapping, fishing, forestry, mining, oil and gas and hydroelectricity. For these industries, *consolidation* is the key. In the future, we can expect that the same goods will be produced with fewer people than in the past. Mines and fish plants will have to automate their production in order to afford to meet strict emissions and other environmental standards that have to be met as the first priority, and to remain competitive in international markets. This will mean fewer rather than more jobs in primary production in these established industries.

This lost employment can be compensated for, in part (but only in part), by concentrating on stronger linkages to the resource industries producing more things for these industries and doing more secondary processing within Labrador itself. For example, the Economic Recovery Commission has been cooperating with the mining companies in western Labrador to hold supplier development forums, where small-scale local manufacturers and suppliers can learn to produce goods and services consumed by the mining operations. In coastal Labrador, government agencies and private sector interests have begun to invest in secondary processing of fish.

While sound environmental management, consolidation and maximizing spin-off benefits are the keys to successful sustainable development in the established resource industries, creativity, imagination and innovation are the keys to developing *new resource industries.* We need to broaden what we *mean* by resource industries to include anything available in nature for which human demand exceeds, or can potentially exceed, supply. For example, the clean water of the brooks of Labrador could be used as the basis of a bottled water industry; ice from icebergs could be harvested for sale as environmentally pure ice in metropolitan markets. Alternative energy sources such as peat and wind could be harnessed as commercial resources. Labrador also has potential for agrifoods and aquacultural development. Environmental concerns must take precedence, from the outset, in the development of these new resource industries.

The pristine natural environment of Labrador and other northern regions can itself be viewed as a new natural resource, or set of resources fresh air, clean water, wide-open spaces, attractive scenery, plentiful fish and game that can be managed for controlled economic development. Protecting such resources makes environmental sense, but it also makes economic sense. In order that the economic benefits of these resources be realized, it is essential that massive industrialization *not* be allowed to occur in Labrador and similar peripheral regions in the north.

It also makes sense to think about maximizing spin-off benefits from these new resource industries from the outset. Training of guides, provisioning of tourists, manufacturing equipment, the aim should be to capture as much of this economic activity as possible within Labrador itself.

It must also be recognized, however, that resource industries by themselves will not provide the wealth and employment that Labradorians will need in the future. A strategy for sustainable development in the periphery must include a concerted effort to *diversify* the regional economy away from too great a dependency on resource industries. Again, this makes both good *economic* sense, the resource industries cannot generate the levels of income and employment the regions need; and good *environmental* sense, the pressures on the environment are lessened to the extent that resource exploitation becomes less important in the regional economy.

New, Knowledge-Based Industries. In a small community on the coast of Labrador, an American with computer and communications knowledge, has become a new kind of local entrepreneur. His company, Wilderness Software, does programming and data processing for large public and private sector clients located in St. John's and other larger centres. Since his costs of production are comparable to urban rates, and transportation is not a factor in this industry, Wilderness Software is managing to compete successfully with urban-based firms.

In the future, the economies of peripheral regions will have to *diversify* into non-resource-based industries ensuring that local people are knowledgeable about modern telecommunications can help make this happen. In Ireland, many rural communities have been given a new lease on life by becoming involved in information industries, the fastest growing sector of the economy internationally. Information industries can provide jobs at various points on the occupational spectrum in rural just as well as in urban areas. Local service bureaus, where workers convert manual into computerized data for multinational corporations, have succeeded in Ireland and they can succeed in Labrador and northern Europe as well. These provide low-skill routine jobs, but so does the local fish plant; and the service bureaus have the advantages of more pleasant working conditions and year-round employment. Companies like Wilderness Software show that it is also possible to develop more sophisticated information industry employment in remote rural communities.

Modern telecommunications is the key to this kind of economic diversification. In recognition of this, the federal government through the Atlantic Provinces Opportunities Agency and the provincial government through Enterprise Newfoundland and Labrador Corporation recently established the ACOA\Enterprise Network. This is a telecommunications network that, once fully established, will allow people in all parts of the province to have immediate access to up-to-date information on business opportunities, government support programs, training programs, market trends and other sorts of information needed for business success. The idea is to *level the playing field* for rural businesses so that they can compete successfully in provincial, national and international markets.

Diversification into adventure tourism, information industries and other service sector activity not only provides employment, but it also helps protect the environment. The greater the diversification, the lesser the pressure on resource industries to provide the economic growth that people yearn for. Well-educated, knowledgeable people are the key to such diversification.

Household Production and Income Security. Household production entails members of a household producing goods and services either for their own consumption or for that of other local households on an informal exchange basis. Economists are now recognizing that such activities produce real wealth and have real economic value. People living in the northern peripheries, both natives and white settlers, have long recognized this although they have been unable, until now, to give theoretical legitimation to such economic activities. Building and repairing one's own house, gathering firewood for home heating, hunting or fishing for food for household consumption, providing baby sitting services for a neighbour and a host of other activities all contribute to household well-being.

Such activities need to be recognized and encouraged. The point to emphasize here is that new forms of knowledge and technology can lead to greater productivity and real wealth creation within the household economy as well as in the market economy, for example in building energy efficient houses. The new economy in the periphery should emphasize the role of knowledge in the household economy.

The non-cash, household economy should not, however, be romanticized. Indeed, a successful modern household economy depends crucially on the cash economy. Money is needed to buy tools, materials, fuels and various services that make for a vibrant household economy. In some poor native communities in Labrador, the amount of money coming into households is so low that the household economy is undermined. The rural economy is best thought of as a nexus of market and non-market elements.[3]

The need for cash underlines another feature of the economies of the northern peripheries of advanced industrial countries: they have become firmly embedded in the institutions of the modern welfare state, and households are typically dependent on state transfers for a significant proportion of their cash incomes.

Despite neo-conservative pressures to cut back on income support to needy families, the social consensus in Canada and Scandinavia continues to hold that the state should play a redistributive role to bring household incomes up to at least a minimal level.

Unfortunately, the types of income security systems that have evolved in western countries over the years have been geared mainly to the needs and conditions of citizens living in the industrial south. The rules and regulations governing income support are often inappropriate in the north and can inhibit rather than support locally based economic development. In Canada, for example, the rules governing unemployment insurance discriminate against self-employment and discourage seasonal employees from working or pursuing their education during the off-season. In Newfoundland and Labrador, efforts are currently underway to reform the income security system to make it more suitable to the needs of people living in rural communities.[4] Again, *knowledge* is the key to redesigning income security so that it contributes to sustainable development in the north. Realistically, national states have to recognize that people living in the north will continue to rely on income support for part of their cash income for many years to come. The challenge is not to reduce the support, but rather to reform it so that it contributes to rather than impedes economic activity.

5. Conclusion: An Agency of Change?

Adam Smith looked to the bourgeoisie to overthrow the last vestiges of feudal society to establish market society; Karl Marx hoped that the proletariat would be the social class to lead society to the next stage of evolution, socialism; and political thinkers in the twentieth century have depended on various social agents the intelligentsia, the peasantry, students, women depending on their point of view, to be the harbingers of progressive social change.

But practical experience and commonsense suggest that no one social grouping can be identified as *the* agency of change. Take the incredible changes that have occurred in the Soviet Union and Eastern Europe in the past couple of years for example. They were not the result of the efforts of any single social class or group but rather the collective outcome of many social forces built on a kind of consensus of knowledge, knowledge that a centrally planned economy on a massive scale is simply incapable of *delivering the goods* nearly as effectively as a market economy.

To achieve knowledge-based, sustainable development in the north, we need not an agency of change, but rather many *agents of change* located throughout the social system, in the environmental movement, in the universities, in local communities, in native people's organizations, in labour unions, in business associations and in government. The fight has to be fought on many fronts, with patience but also with diligence. We need a knowledgeable population and knowledgeable decision-makers who come to understand that, in the long run, sustainable development is in everybody's best interests. The way in which we choose to develop our northern peripheries over the next 10 to 20 years *can* become a model of how to develop the global economy for a sustainable future.

Notes

1. For more elaborate discussions of the political economy and sociology of Labrador see House (1986).
2. Human ecologists include Marx himself with his insistence on the primacy of "man-nature" relationships and the Chicago school of sociology early in this century.
3. For an initial effort to formalize a model of the household economy, see Appendix IV of *Building on Our Strengths*, the Report of the Royal Commission on Employment and Unemployment (1986).
4. For an initial attempt at this, see Chapter 12 of the 1986 Newfoundland and Labrador Royal Commission Report entitled 'A New Income Security System'.

References

Government of Newfoundland and Labrador, 1986. *Building on Our Strengths*. Report of the Royal Commission on Employment and Unemployment.

House, J. D., 1980. 'Coastal Labrador: Incorporation, Exploitation and Underdevelopment'. *The Journal of Canadian Studies*, No. 15, pp. 98-113.

Polanyi, Karl, 1944. *The Great Transformation.* New York: Farrar and Rinehart.

9 Financial resources for sustainable development in the Arctic

Michael Pretes

1. Introduction

Achieving economic development in peripheral regions such as the Arctic has long been a difficult problem. Dependence on natural resource extraction, together with an absence of direct economic control, has only increased the marginality of these regions. Other factors, such as distance from markets and high transportation costs, have added to the problem. Diversification programs have been largely unsuccessful, in many cases due to lack of adequate funding. These features of peripheral regions have tended to increase their reliance on resource extraction for export.

The current concept of *sustainable development* has been of great interest to peripheral regions, as research on sustainable development has focused on the problems of marginal areas. The literature is still not in agreement about just what constitutes sustainable development, but generally the concept is deemed to include compatibility between economic and social activity and the environment, a shift towards renewable resource use, decentralization and local control of resources, equitable distribution of resource wealth, and an emphasis on economic *activity*, rather than economic *growth*.

These components of sustainable development have particular meaning in the Arctic. But most Arctic development to date has been strictly contrary to the above: it has been largely in the form of mega-projects and large-scale industries with little environmental concern. Examples include the petroleum projects and pipelines in Alaska, mining and industrial complexes on the Kola Peninsula and at Norilsk in the USSR, large-scale mining developments in Greenland, and hydroelectric projects in Canada and Scandinavia.

Non-renewable resources are and will continue to be the engine of development in northern regions for many years. This is not necessarily the best form of development, but in many cases political and social circumstances require such projects. While a shift away from dependence on these resources is desirable from a sustainable development perspective, this shift is not likely to take place for some time. Two aspects of resource use are suggested: a move away from mega-projects and towards small-scale resource developments, and the utilization of natural resource rents to effect changes in the economic base. This latter aspect is the subject of this article.

2. Problems of Finance Capital

This article assumes that the implementation of sustainable development initiatives is a desirable alternative to the industrial projects that have characterized Arctic development. Why haven't such initiatives materialized on a large scale, despite growing environmental pressure and the long-term economic and ecological benefits? The fundamental problem is financing such initiatives. The circumpolar Arctic is an economic colony of developed southern metropolitan regions, and as such is underdeveloped and exploited. Private, external capital is reluctant to finance sustainable development initiatives, partly because of the greater risk involved, and partly because the economic returns, especially to the financier, are limited. Hence outside capital has historically demonstrated a lack of interest in the Arctic, with occasional funding reserved for mega-projects only. Most of these mega-projects are concerned with large-scale energy and mineral resource extraction, activities that are capital intensive, unsustainable, and have a negative environmental impact.

2.1 Problems of Dependency

The Arctic is peripheral to metropolitan political, financial and manufacturing centres, and serves as a resource-producing hinterland of metropolitan regions. Capital generation in these hinterlands is difficult, and thus the hinterland must rely on capital imported from the centre. The problems of capital formation in the periphery have been analyzed by the dependency school of development. Frank (1969), argues that the metropolis-satellite system, characteristic of centre-periphery relations, keeps peripheral development dependent on development in the centre. Frank notes that the world's peripheral regions have been incorporated into the world economy since the colonial period. This incorporation has transformed the peripheral economies from their indigenous state into that of the colonizing power. These close links between centre and periphery develop into a hierarchical relationship in which the periphery, or satellite, becomes dependent on the centre for capital and finished goods. The periphery functions as a resource-exporting region in which economic rent is transferred to the centre (see Figure 9.1). According to Frank, a weakening of the metropolitan-satellite ties stimulates the opportunities for development of the periphery.

The general ideas elaborated by Frank are shared by many dependency scholars. Many scholars agree that peripheral development is not autonomous, but is closely linked to external actions emanating from the centre. Capital flows from centre to periphery do not lead to development in the periphery, but rather to a continued state of dependence on such flows. Wallerstein (1974) replaces the issue of internal and external causes of underdevelopment by conceptualizing a world economy composed of core states, semi-periphery, periphery, and external arena. Galtung (1971) adapts the Frank model of metropolis-satellite to one of penetration and fragmentation. Galtung's model is particularly useful in that it recognizes non-economic factors in peripheralization, such as communications, culture, and power. The solution to underdevelopment, in the eyes of many dependency and neo-dependency scholars, is to reform the ties between centre and periphery, thus allowing the peripheral areas to establish their own political and economic policies and to develop their resources for their own benefit. When applied to the Arctic – or any other peripheral region for that matter – this argument suggests that the periphery needs greater political and economic autonomy, and that external capital must be regulated and limited.

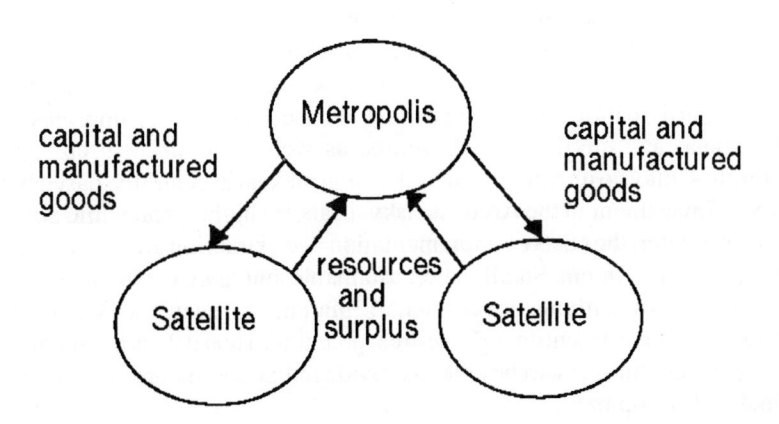

Figure 9.1 The Relationship Between Metropolis and Satellite. Adapted from Frank (1969)

Greater economic autonomy is closely tied to the generation of capital. External capital, even if it were to fund sustainable development initiatives, is itself not sustainable. The provision of external capital is based on investment: the financier expects to receive a significant financial return, a return greater than similar investments in southern regions, to compensate for risk. Since most private capital is externally based, any potential revenues or rents are likely to leave the Arctic, finding their way instead to the metropolitan capital centres of the south. Moreover, Arctic residents have little or no control over the use of external capital; political, as well as economic, power is in most cases extremely limited. Hence external capital is not a panacea for the development problems of the Arctic.

2.2 Sources of New Capital

Where will local sources of capital in the Arctic come from? The record for retaining and reinvesting local capital in the circumpolar Arctic is extremely poor, leading to the Arctic's continuing dependence on capital from the south. Banks, private corporations, and national governments have been historical sources of finance capital, but few are indigenous, and most are concerned with resource extraction for southern or national interests. New funds from native land claims settlements are a possible source of new capital, but generally are limited to specific groups.

There are few if any indigenous banks in the circumpolar North. In the Soviet Union all capital was controlled by a single central bank based in Moscow. Canada has no indigenous northern banks or trust companies; all northern capital is controlled by the five southern banks based in Toronto and Montréal. Alaska does have a few locally-based banks, but many of these are subsidiaries of larger banking chains in the western USA. And in Scandinavia most banks are based in Oslo, Stockholm, or Helsinki. The fact that banks are externally controlled limits the policy participation of local residents, whose interests are unrepresented. Unique social and environmental factors, as well as unique entrepreneurial opportunities, may go unrecognized by decision makers in centrally-based banks. Moreover, investment in the Arctic is risky: costs are higher, and while potential returns are greater, the costs of implementation and extraction are often much too high to justify investment. Small scale, sustainable, but risky ventures are usually ignored by banks without governmental guarantees, even though, by local standards, such investments may have great potential. Thus it does not seem likely that banking institutions will be able to provide indigenous sources of capital for sustainable development.

Private corporations have contributed much of the new capital for Arctic development. But private investment is clearly self-interested: the proper role of the corporation under capitalism is to maximize profit for the shareholders. Augmenting the social good is not a corporate goal unless such an augmentation would assist in the attainment of corporate goals. Since most corporations are based outside of the Arctic, and have very few Arctic residents as shareholders, they favour policies that will benefit southern interests. In general, private corporations have no objection to state-sponsored development programmes if these do not inhibit corporate functions or reduce the ability of the corporation to generate a profit. Furthermore, most private investment in the Arctic is short-term. Most resource extractive projects have a limited life and depend on economic and price cycles. The private firm is not likely to provide capital sources for local residents. Most private firms are engaged in resource extraction. Such forms of investment may provide short-term benefits, such as employment, for local residents, but they do not aid the long-term formation of local capital, which is the key to peripheral development.

Additional sources of Arctic capital can be found, in some areas, through native land claims settlements. At present, native groups in North America are negotiating settlements involving land transfers and large cash payments in exchange for surrendering certain existing and pending claims. Some claims have already been settled. The Alaska Native Claims Settlement Act of 1971 extinguished all outstanding native claims to land and to hunting and fishing rights in exchange for a non-taxable compensation payment of $962.5 million, paid over ten years. Native groups were also entitled to select 44 million acres of land to be held in fee simple, including sub-surface rights. The land transfers and compensation payments were paid to twelve regional corporations and one additional corporation representing non-resident natives. The cash compensation, paid the federal government, injected new capital into Alaska and especially into the hands of local residents, allowing them to finance their own ventures.

The James Bay and Northern Quebec Agreement of 1975 paid $225 million (Canadian) over a twenty year period to the Cree and Inuit of northern Quebec, in exchange for extinguishment of aboriginal title. The Inuvialuit Final Agreement of 1984 will give over $152 million (Canadian) to the Inuvialuit of northwestern Canada in exchange for a similar renunciation of title. The Council of Yukon Indians, the Dene-Métis, and the Tungavik Federation of Nunavut (representing the Inuit of the eastern Canadian Arctic) all have pending claims. Collectively cash compensation for the three outstanding claims could total as much as $4 billion, depending on payment schedules and interest rates (Robinson et al. 1989). Although this money will be paid to native groups it will affect the overall economy through purchases and investments. Hence, in some areas, land claim settlements could inject large sums of money into the regional economy and provide a source of local capital. But it must be remembered that native land claims settlements involve compensation, money in payment for an earlier loss. Payments are restricted to native residents, though indirect benefits often extend to the entire community. Native land claims settlements will provide new sources of investment capital, but will apply only in certain situations.

Governments will continue to play a major role in northern economies. To take but one example, the Government of the Northwest Territories in Canada accounts for 29% of total jobs, and 35% of total wages in the territory, compared to a 9% of total jobs and 12% of total wages in Canada as a whole (Special Committee on the Northern Economy 1988). The public sector accounts for 55% of the territorial domestic product (Patterson 1988). The small and thinly spread out population of the territory, the lack of adequate infrastructure and the high costs of resource extraction limit the tax base and potential revenue sources of the territorial government, while also increasing the costs of service implementation. The Government of the Northwest Territories is therefore dependent on the Government of Canada for 84% of its budget. National governments are important sources of finance in many northern areas. But as the above figures reflect, much of this financial support is needed to fund social services and administration.

Most northern regions – with the exception of Alaska and the partial exception of Greenland – are under direct national government control, and these national governments control the extraction of natural resources. National governments often view the resources of the periphery, and especially of the Arctic, as resources to be used for the benefit of the entire nation. Hence national policies are often unresponsive to local interests, and Arctic residents have little input into national decision-making, as the regional population is small. Moreover, national fund transfers are not sustainable, because they depend on national economic conditions and policies, and northern development is not accorded a high priority. Arctic regions are economic colonies of the developed south, and increasingly depend on national government support payments, as the statistics from the Northwest Territories show. Furthermore, government activity exhibits a collusive relationship with private capital, often supporting the entry of private capital, for example by granting permission for protected areas to be opened up to resource exploration and extraction, and by financing the necessary infrastructure, such as roads and airstrips. This collusive relationship permeates economic cycles: during periods of expansion and growth the government also expands and increases services, while during periods of decline and stagnation the government likewise contracts, hence increasing the impact of economic boom and bust cycles. National governments cannot be expected to finance and encourage sustainable initiatives.

2.3 Transition Stage

An alternative solution – and perhaps the only solution – is to develop indigenous sources of capital in the Arctic. A local capital base would be more conducive to regional interests, and would not rely upon outside investment decisions. Furthermore, any revenues or rents generated by local capital investment would remain within the region. Hence local capital is preferable on two grounds: 1) it is locally controlled and investment decisions are made locally, taking into account local interests and social and environmental concerns; and 2) any profits or rents will remain within the region, rather than migrating outside. Hence the economic benefits will accrue to local people, rather than to external financiers.

Local sources of investment capital can be created through a transformation of the Arctic's own natural resources. The Arctic has potential in non-renewable, renewable, and human resources. The latter two are preferable from a sustainable development perspective, since, in Schumacher's (1974) view they are analogous to living on interest, rather than on principal. Certainly an Arctic economy based on renewable resources (such as forestry, fish, reindeer, and agriculture) and human resources (such as tourism, small-scale manufacturing, and service industries) is preferable from both an ecological and social perspective, in that it places less stress on environment and society. In order to generate capital to fund such an economy, however, the Arctic must first pass through a transition stage, in which non-renewable resources are used to generate investment capital. Non-renewable resources are responsible for both maintaining employment and creating investment capital during the transition stage.

Table 9.1
Characteristics of Present, Transition Stage, and Future Peripheral Economies

Factor	Present	Transition	Future
resource base	non-renewable	non-renewable	renewable
resource use	export	export	local
resource processing	external	external	local
resource rents	migrate	trust fund	local use
project initiation	external	external/internal	internal
project scale	large	large	small
project life	short	short	long
project authority	external	local	local
education level	low	high	high
employment duration	short	short	long
employment type	primary	primary	tertiary
social participation	limited	active	active
capital sources	external	external	trust fund
environmental controls	national	national	local

The transition stage is the period in which the structure of the region's economy is transformed from a largely industrial, mega-project-oriented, non-renewable resource-extracting economy to that approximating a sustainable, small industry-based, renewable resource dependent economy. This change might also be characterized as a shift from modernism to post-modernism (Faragó 1991). During the transition stage non-renewable resource industries will be important as generators of investment capital to fund the post-modern economy. Table 9.1 indicates some of the basic characteristics of the present, transition, and future stages of the regional economy. Steps to implement the transition stage should be taken immediately. It is impossible, given social constraints (such as employment) to instantly abandon existing resource extraction. Except in areas where other sources of local capital can be found, non-renewable resources will constitute the principal source of investment capital. While these industries must conform to acceptable environmental standards, they are necessary to generate local capital. Using the mechanism of a permanent trust fund, non-renewable resource extraction can generate investment capital during the transition stage, preparing the way for the future sustainable economy based on renewable resources, services, and minimal industry.

3. Permanent Trust Funds

Much of the Arctic periphery depends on the extraction of petroleum and minerals – resources that are inherently depletable and unsustainable. These resources are likely to see continued exploitation, especially as they are connected to national economic and security interests (Critchley 1986). How can these resources contribute to sustainable development in the Arctic? The key is in transforming mineral and petroleum resources into renewable financial resources. Permanent trust funds (a type of investment and development fund) can be used to make this transformation from mineral and petroleum resources to investment and business development (Pretes, forthcoming; Pretes and Robinson 1989). Permanent trust funds also assist in decentralizing the economy. These funds have been successfully used in parts of North America, where such regions as Alaska and Alberta have saved resource revenues and have lessened their dependence on the central government. Alaska, for example, now has a permanent trust fund with a balance of more than $12 billion, most of which was saved from the sale of petroleum. The fund produces an annual income of over $1 billion, which helps to finance the Alaska economy.

Permanent trust funds are special state-controlled accounts in which the principal is protected from expenditure by the government. The funds derive their principal, or capital, from revenues received through the export sale of the state's natural resources. Rather than spending these revenues directly, the revenues are instead channelled into a permanent trust fund where the capital can increase through investment. As the capital increases both through deposits and investment income, additional funds become available. The original fund capital can be preserved while the fund income can be used to fund sustainable development initiatives, and to diversify the economy away from non-renewable resource dependence during the transition stage. In this way the capital is never depleted, and the fund itself becomes a renewable resource. Minerals and petroleum are depletable resources, but the permanent trust fund can exist in perpetuity. Income from the trust fund can replace resource income as resource production declines. Eventually financial investment could be a major source of income for a region (see Figure 9.2). Permanent trust funds are distinct from developmental funds, the capital of which is generated by various sources and allocated by the government through its general fund. Permanent trust fund capital does not, in most cases, pass through the general fund. Fund capital has specific, distinct sources and specific, distinct uses, and, moreover, the fund is protected from government intervention.

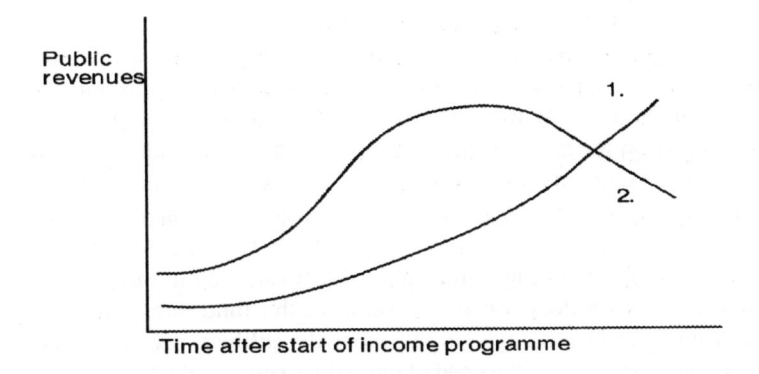

Figure 9.2 The Relationship Between Permanent Trust Fund Income (1) and Non-Renewable Resource Income (2)

Permanent trust funds can serve several functions. They can 1) save resource revenues that might otherwise be spent; 2) extend the benefits of resource income over several generations or in perpetuity; 3) provide an additional source of income for the region; 4) be used to intervene in the regional economy to promote economic diversification or ensure environmental standards; 5) decentralize the economy by providing local sources of capital; and 6) externalize windfalls and prevent distortions in the economy.

Trust funds are based on the principle that future generations should share in the revenues obtained from resources extracted in the present. By isolating revenues in a trust fund, the revenues are saved and can be used to meet future needs. The funds also isolate revenues from immediate government spending, and thus alter the resources available for immediate use. In this way economic cycles can be modified, for the fund can save a greater portion of rents during periods of economic prosperity, and retain less during periods of economic stagnation. The fund thus moderates the boom and bust cycles that characterize peripheral resource-based economies. Natural resources prices fall and rise in a free market. Therefore a regional economy can experience a massive increase of windfall resource revenues during periods of high demand and high prices. Such huge inflows of revenue can have a major effect on a small economy. In most cases the economy is unable to absorb these rents, and much is wasted. Increasing prosperity also leads to increased expectations that linger even when economic prosperity ends. By depositing a portion of these windfall, excess revenues in a trust fund, the problems of absorption can be largely avoided. The economic rents become sterilized, and, if the fund invests outside the region, become externalized. These externalized rents can be slowly reintegrated into the regional economy at a controlled pace during periods of stagnation and recession. And by providing a local source of capital, the trust fund reduces the need for external capital and helps to decentralize the economy.

The flow of revenues through a model trust fund is indicated in Figure 9.3. This model is that used by the Alaska Permanent Fund. The resource revenues, together with any additional monies saved by the state (special appropriations), pass into the main permanent fund account, and form the principal. Fund earnings, resulting from investments in stocks, bonds, and real estate, pass into the Earnings Reserve Account (ERA), where they are temporarily held until the state authorizes expenditure. The principal remains unspent, but the ERA acts as an expendable holding account. The ERA is divided into three parts: part of the money is retained in the fund as earnings, part of it is returned to the principal where it protects against a decrease in the value of the fund due to inflation (inflation-proofing), and the remainder is paid out to the public as dividends. This model satisfies several demands: the need of the state to save for the future (when resources are depleted), generation of income, protection of the fund principal against inflation, restrictions on fund expenditure to avoid the fund being controlled by political interest groups, and direct payments to local residents to stimulate purchasing power and to allow residents to make their own investment decisions. The dividends also release new venture capital into the economy. By regulating the entry of capital into the economy, both through the dividends and through investments, the state can moderate the economic boom and bust cycles by limiting the distorting impacts of windfalls.

The permanent trust fund can invest saved capital in both structural and financial investments. Structural projects are designed to reflect environmental and social concerns, provide employment in the region, and increase the standard of living. The criteria used in selecting projects are largely social and environmental, and have been employed extensively in the case of the Alberta Heritage Savings Trust Fund (AHSTF) in Canada. By redirecting capital, the state can encourage diversification of the economy through investments in other, non-

Financial resources for sustainable development in the Arctic 103

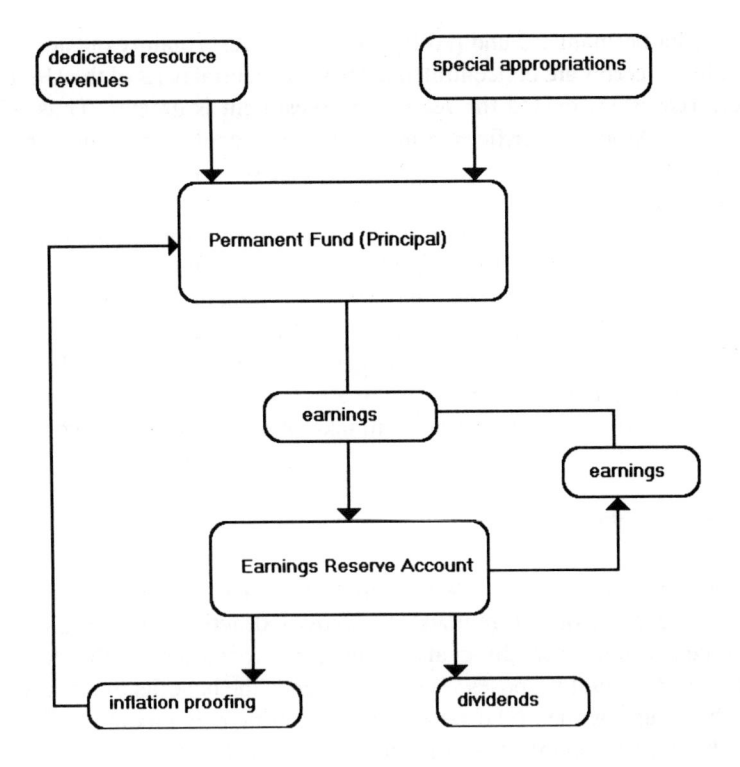

Figure 9.3 A Sample Trust Fund Structure. The Structure Shown is that of the Alaska Permanent Fund

resource, sectors. In Alberta, fund capital has also been invested in new forms of resource technology, as in, for example, extraction of petroleum from shale and tar sands. A venture capital fund has been established with fund capital to support technology and medical industries. Irrigation projects, rail hopper cars, a grain terminal, rural telephone service, parks and recreation areas, and hospitals have also been funded with AHSTF capital. The state has argued that most of these projects would not have been carried out if the AHSTF did not exist. The AHSTF balance currently stands at over $12 billion (Canadian), with additional deemed assets of over $3 billion (Canadian) (Alberta Heritage Savings Trust Fund 1990). Deemed assets consist of infrastructure that does not produce a direct economic return.

Financial investment may be carried out outside of the region; investments include stocks, bonds, and real estate. Financial criteria are used in selecting investments. The financial investments provide an annual income that increases the value of the permanent trust fund, and thus increases the amount of capital available for social purposes. This latter form of investment has been pursued by the Alaska Permanent Fund (APF). The APF invests mainly outside of Alaska. Most investments are concentrated in the more central parts of the United States, where risk is lower and the return on investment is greater. Thus Alaska, in contrast to Alberta, sacrifices immediate social benefits for long-term financial benefits that will aid future generations. But the state does not neglect immediate concerns: approximately half of the income generated by the APF is paid out directly to Alaskan residents in the form of annual dividends. The APF fund balance stands at over $12 billion (US), and the 1990 dividend payment was $952.63 to each Alaskan resident (Alaska Permanent Fund 1991).

An important concern in the management of the permanent trust fund is the retention of principal. As the name suggests, the fund is intended to be permanent. In this manner the benefits of resource extraction are extended across many generations, since all generations will take part in using fund income.

4. Conclusion

Permanent trust funds are a resource management option for peripheral regions that are dependent on non-renewable resource extraction. By saving and isolating resource revenues from direct and immediate expenditure by the state, the trust fund serves several purposes. The fund extends the benefits of resource income into the future, while at the same time generating new income to finance state activity and sustainable development initiatives. The fund also provides local capital for investment, and moderates economic cycles by controlling the entry of capital into the market.

Permanent trust funds are a useful strategy for achieving sustainable development in the Arctic region. During the transition stage to a truly sustainable economy, non-renewable resources can be harnessed to generate the needed investment capital. If Arctic regions are given control over their own resources and their own trust funds, then each region can develop its own capital source to finance local development. Moreover, a fund will be in place when resources are depleted. The establishment of a permanent trust fund – in conjunction with devolution of authority to regions – will allow both a greater degree of independence and decentralization, and a local capital source that can be used to implement sustainable development.

References

Alaska Permanent Fund, 1991. *Annual Report*. Juneau, Alaska.
Alberta Heritage Savings Trust Fund, 1990. *Quarterly Investment Report* (September 30). Edmonton.
Critchley, H., 1986. 'The economic and human resources of the Arctic', in

L'arctique: espace stratégique vital pour les grandes puissances. Québec: Centre québécois de relations internationales, Université Laval.

Faragó, L., 1991. 'Postmodernism: the critique of modernization or a new challenge'. Paper presented at the Regional Science Association European Congress, Lisbon, Portugal, 27-30 August.

Frank, A. G., 1969. *Capitalism and underdevelopment in Latin America: historical studies of Chile and Brazil.* New York: Monthly Review Press.

Galtung, J., 1971. 'A structural theory of imperialism', *Journal of Peace Research,* Vol. 8, No. 2.

Patterson, D., 1988. 'Political and economic realities in the Northwest Territories', *Arcana Poli,* Vol. 1, No. 1.

Pretes, M. (forthcoming). *The problem of wealth: natural resource management and trust funds.* Calgary.

Pretes, M. and Robinson, M., 1989. 'Beyond boom and bust: a strategy for sustainable development in the North', *Polar Record,* Vol. 25, No. 153.

Robinson, M., Dickerson, M., Van Camp, J., Wuttunee, W., Pretes, M. and Binder, L., 1989. *Coping with the cash: a financial review of four northern land claims settlements with a view to maximizing economic opportunities from the next generation of claims settlements in the Northwest Territories.* Yellowknife: Special Committee on the Northern Economy, Legislative Assembly of the Northwest Territories.

Schumacher, E. F., 1974. *Small is beautiful.* London: Sphere Books.

Special Committee on the Northern Economy, 1988. *Workshop on the northern economy: summary of presentations.* Yellowknife, Canada: Legislative Assembly of the Northwest Territories.

Wallerstein, I., 1974. *The modern world-system: capitalist agriculture and the origins of the European world-economy in the sixteenth century.* New York: Academic Press.

Index

aboriginal peoples 27
acid rain 17, 38-40, 43, 44, 49, 65
Adler-Karlsson, Gunnar 15, 18, 20, 21, 24
aerosols 36, 37, 49
Agranat, G. A. 29-32
agricultural society 15
Alaska 3, 8, 11, 13, 14, 32, 35, 51, 53-55, 57, 58, 60, 64, 81, 93, 96-98, 100, 102-104
Alberta 5, 100, 102-104
Aleutian Chain 53
Amazonia 8
Amin, Samir 14, 20, 21, 24
Anaya, S. J. 64
Andalusia 8
Anders, Gary C. 11, 13
Anders, Kathleen K. 11, 13
Andreyeva, E. 28, 29, 31, 32
Antarctic 11, 36, 39, 40, 43, 48
Antarctica 10, 14, 40, 46
Appalachia 8, 9, 14
Aral Sea 16
Archer, Clive 45, 47
Arctic 1-3, 8, 11, 19, 24-27, 29-33, 35-49, 51, 54-57, 62, 63, 65, 67, 76, 78, 79, 82, 83, 93-100, 104
Arctic Circle 67
Arctic Council 62
Arctic haze 2, 35-49, 55
Arkin, William M. 57, 65
armed security 20, 22, 23
Arrighi, Giovanni 7, 13

Bantustans 8
Barrie, Leonard A. 36-38, 47, 48
Barsh, R. 64
Batteau, Allen 10, 14
Beaufort Sea 54, 55

Benedict, Richard 38, 48
Berger, T. R. 53, 65
Bering Strait 27
Berman, M. 70, 78
biosphere 13, 20, 21
Blue Nile 58
Borough 11, 64
Brezhnev, Leonid 44
Brundtland Commission 15
Brundtland Report 16, 18, 24, 60, 65, 70, 77, 84

California 9
Canada 7, 8, 11, 29, 40, 42, 45, 46, 55-58, 60, 63-65, 81, 83, 89, 94, 96-98, 102, 105
Capra, F. 71, 78
Carey, John 35, 48
Caribbean 7, 9, 14
centralization 18, 20, 21, 70
Chernobyl 55, 77
Chicago 9, 90
China 7, 8, 14
Chukchi Sea 54
Chukotka 29
Churchill Falls 83
Cincinnati 9
Circumpolar North 25, 96
civil security 22, 23
climatic change 38, 48
Cold War 1, 25, 39, 40, 43
Connolly, William E. 15, 20, 24
Copenhagen 47
core 6-10, 12, 13, 54, 69, 79, 95
Cornia, Giovanni A. 9, 14
Corsica 8
Cree 5, 58, 97
Critchley, H. 100, 104
cultural identity 3, 6, 9-11, 13, 17, 19,

107

28, 57, 59, 63, 69-72, 76-79
culture 6, 11, 19, 27, 52, 69-72, 76, 78, 83, 84, 95
cultures 3, 6, 52, 54, 59, 61, 83

Damas, D. 53, 65
Davis Inlet 83
decentralization 30, 93, 104
Dene-Métis 97
dependency 5, 10, 87, 94, 95
Deudney, J. 64
development 1-5, 10, 12, 14-32, 43, 44, 46, 53-55, 58-62, 67, 69, 71, 76-79, 81, 82, 84-87, 89, 90, 93-101, 104, 105
Doolittle, M. 55, 65
dumping 56, 63, 64

East Asian NICs 7, 8
East Bengal 9
Eastern Europe 7, 90
economic activity 3, 7, 9-12, 14-23, 25-30, 32, 36, 44, 53, 58-61, 63, 68, 69, 74, 77, 78, 82-89, 93-105
economic growth 15-18, 20-23, 86, 88, 93
ecosystem 26, 31, 35, 37, 45, 46, 59, 72
environment 2, 3, 16-27, 29-32, 36, 38-41, 43-49, 52-56, 58, 59, 61-65, 71, 72, 77-79, 81, 82, 84, 86-88, 93, 99
environmental catastrophes 16-18
environmental changes 17, 38
environmental damage 28-31
environmental protection 3, 26, 28, 30-32, 43, 58
Eskimo 11
Ethiopia 58
ethnic identity 69
Export Processing Zones 12
Exxon Valdez 54, 55, 58

Faragó, L. 100, 105
Finger, Matthias 18, 24
Finland 7, 21, 30, 36, 40, 42, 43, 45, 67, 68
Finnmark 67, 74, 77, 79
Frank, Andre Gunder 23, 94, 95, 105
Freeman, M. M. R. 71, 78

Gällivare 69
Galtung, J. 95, 105
Geneva 44
German Democratic Republic 16
Germany 8, 16, 57
Ghai, Dharam 9, 14
Ghana 9
Gleick, P. 58, 64, 65
global warming 39, 43, 55
Goldfrank, Walter L. 2, 5, 12, 14, 82
Golubchikov, Yu. 27, 32
Goose Bay 57, 83
Gorbachev, Mikhail 25, 40, 45, 63
Great Britain 17
Griffiths, F. 32
growth-oriented economy 15, 16, 18, 23
Gulf 8, 55, 58
Gulf War 58

Haas, Peter M. 42, 48
Handler, J. 57, 65
Hannum, H. 54, 65
Happy Valley-Goose Bay 83
Hedmark 74
hegemony 7, 8
Heidam, N. Z. 47, 49
Heininen, L. 77, 79
Heintzenberg, Jost 37, 48
Helander, Elina 3, 67, 71, 79
Helsinki 24, 40, 44, 96
Hettne, Björn 15, 17, 20, 24
Hewitt de Alcantara, Cynthia 9, 14
Honko, L. 69, 79

Hopedale 83
Hopson, Eben 64
House, Douglas 3, 24, 81, 88, 90, 91
human rights 53, 54, 59, 61-64
Hurdal 47
Hussein, Saddam 58

identity 17, 27, 28, 69, 70, 76, 79, 83
independence 10, 27, 104
India 8, 13
indians 11, 53, 63-65, 79, 97
indigenous 3, 11-13, 17, 27, 30, 39, 51-54, 58-65, 67, 79, 94, 96, 98
indigenous peoples 3, 12, 17, 27, 39, 51-54, 58-65
indigenous rights 53, 54, 59-61, 63, 64
Indonesia 8
industrial desert 30
industrial expansionism 82, 86
industrial society 15, 39, 82
industrialization 2, 3, 12, 20, 81, 86, 87
infrastructure 9, 29, 54, 98, 103
Innu 57, 81, 83, 84
insecurity 52, 54, 62
International Arctic Science Committee 46, 47, 62
international regime 35, 38, 40, 41
Inuit 11, 39, 51, 52, 56, 58, 59, 62, 64, 81, 83, 97
Inuit Circumpolar Conference 39, 62, 64
Inupiat 11, 14
Inuvialuit 97
Ireland 88
Italy 7, 8
Izvestiya 28

Jackson, C. Ian 40, 44, 48
James Bay 58, 97
Jesperson, Eva 9, 14

Käkönen, Jyrki 1, 15, 20, 24

Kampuchea 8
Karasjok 68, 79
Kautokeino 68, 72-74, 79
Kindt, J. 55, 65
Kiruna 45
Kola 17, 30, 39, 42, 55, 57, 67, 77, 81, 93
Kotlyakov, V. 30, 32
Krasnopolski, B. Kh. 29, 32
Krasnoyarsk 27
Kruse, John A. 11, 14
Kurdistan 8

Labrador 3, 57, 82-91
Labrador City 83
Lapland 30, 32, 45
Lasko, L. N. 76, 79
Latin America 7, 9, 14, 105
Lee, Keekok 20, 24
legal orders 59
Leninist model 13
Lindholm, S. 71, 79
local authorities 27, 28
long cycles 6
long wave 7, 8, 12
Los Angeles 36
Lovozero 67
Lubicon (Cree) Nation 5

MacKenzie, Debora 45, 48
Magadan 27
Makkovik 83
market economy 17, 18, 89, 90
Marx, Karl 6, 82, 89, 90
Mast, R. F. 55, 65
Maxwell, J. 38, 48
mega-project 58, 93, 94, 100
Mendes, Chico 12
metropolis-satellite system 94, 95
Middle East 12
militarization 1, 56, 62
Mische, P. 64

Mitchell, J. Murray Jr. 35, 48
modern world-system 5-7, 105
modernity 7, 24
modernization 2, 3, 15-17, 19, 20, 22, 70, 105
Montréal 38, 65, 96
Morgan, M. 52, 65
Myanmar 8

Nain 83
Nansen, Fridtjof 35
native 3, 11, 13, 25-28, 52-54, 58, 60, 81, 83, 85, 86, 88-90, 96, 97
natural resources 2, 16, 28, 29, 31, 52, 58, 62, 70, 77, 78, 82, 86, 87, 93, 94, 98-100, 102, 105
Nauka i Zhizn 30, 32
Navajo 11
Netherlands 57
New York 9, 14, 24, 36, 48, 49, 65, 78, 91, 105
Newfoundland 3, 83, 85, 88-90
Newman, Monroe 10, 14
Nikitina, Elena N. 46, 48
non-natives 81, 86
non-renewable resources 3, 58, 94, 99-101, 104
Nordic Sami Council 68
Nordland 74
Norilsk 30, 94
North Slope 11, 14, 64
Northern Alberta 3, 5, 7, 25-32, 45, 54, 55, 58, 59, 63, 77, 81, 83, 84, 86-90, 94, 96-98, 105
Northern Europe 3, 7
Norton Sound 51
Norway 17, 40, 42, 43, 45, 47, 55, 67, 68, 72-74, 76, 77
Norwegian Sea 57

Oikawa, K. K. 37, 48
Olson, M. P. 37, 48

OPEC 13
Osherenko, Gail 39, 48
Oslo 36, 44, 76, 79, 96
Østreng, Willy 39, 46, 48
Ottawa 64, 83, 84
ozone layer 38, 55, 65

Pacific 12
Pakistan 8-10
Parriott, T. 55, 65
Patterson, D. 98, 105
periphery 2-13, 20, 21, 23, 76, 78, 79, 81, 83, 87-90, 93-95, 97-100, 102, 104
permafrost 30, 38, 55
Peterson, N. 57, 65
Pika, A. 27, 32
Point Barrow 35
Poland 16, 45
Polanyi, Karl 12, 82, 91
pollutants 30, 35-37, 39, 40, 42, 44-46, 55, 56
post-modernism 100
Pretes, Michael 3, 78, 79, 93, 100, 105
Prokhorov, B. 27, 32
property right 28, 73

Quebec 57, 58, 64, 86, 97

Rahn, Kenneth A. 36-38, 47, 49
regime 3, 7, 16, 17, 35, 36, 38-47, 57, 59
reindeer herding 27, 31, 37, 67, 72-75, 77, 99
Renaissance 20, 21
renewable resources 3, 58, 94, 99, 100, 104
Resolute 46
resource management 2, 6, 9-11, 13, 25, 26, 28-30, 48, 54, 58, 60, 62, 65, 72, 76, 81, 82, 84-88, 93-105
Rhode Island 47

Rio de Janeiro 43
Ritter, Kathleen V. 11, 14
Robinson, M. 78, 79, 97, 100, 105
Roginko, Alexei Yu. 2, 3, 17, 24-26, 33, 40, 49
Roots, F. 55, 65
Rosh, Robert M. 10, 14
Rovaniemi 32, 36, 44-46
Rovaniemi process 44-46
Ruong, I. 69, 79
Russia 1, 2, 7, 25, 28, 31, 32, 40, 45, 55, 65, 67, 68, 77

Sadat, Anwar 58
Sambo, Dalee 3, 51
Sami people 3, 67-69, 73, 74, 76-79
Samithing 68
Sara, M. N. 72, 79
Sardinia 8
Sarmela, Matti 19-21, 24
Scandinavia 8, 44, 55, 81, 89, 94, 96
Schumacher, E. F. 99, 105
semi-peripheral 6, 8, 10, 12, 13
semi-periphery 6-8, 10, 12, 13, 95
Semipalatinski 16
settlers 9, 11, 83, 85, 88
Shaw, Glenn E. 35, 37, 49
Sheshashit 83
Shlikhter, S. B. 30, 32
Siberia 17, 37, 55
Siberian 26
Sicily 8
Smallwood 85
Smith, Adam 55, 65, 89
Smolicz, J. 69, 79
socialist systems 17
Soroos, Marvin S. 2, 35
South Africa 7
South Asia 7
South Korea 7
Southeast Asia 7
Soviet Union 1, 2, 10, 16, 17, 24-28, 31, 33, 37, 40, 44, 45, 57, 68, 81, 82, 90, 96
St. John's 83, 84, 88
Stockholm 40, 43, 79, 96
Stonehouse, B. 47, 49
sub-Saharan Africa 7, 13
sustainable development 1-4, 15, 16, 18, 19, 21-23, 58, 67, 71, 77-79, 81, 82, 84-87, 89, 90, 93, 94, 96, 99-101, 104, 105
sustainable security 51, 59, 62, 63

Taiwan 6
Thomas, Clive 9, 14
Toronto 47, 65, 79, 96
toxic wastes 42
tradition 3, 20, 27, 67-69, 71, 75, 79
traditional life-style 27, 70
traditional rights 60
traditional societies 19
tributary societies 19
Troms 74
Trøndelag 74
trust fund 3, 99-105
Turkey 7
Tyumen 27

underdevelopment 91, 95, 105
unemployment 5, 11, 21, 27, 83, 86, 89, 90
United Kingdom 45, 57
United Nations 24, 36, 38, 43, 44, 49, 55, 60, 61, 64
urbanization 18, 20
USA 7-9, 29, 42, 64, 96
USSR 8, 23, 25, 31, 32, 42, 63, 64, 94

Varmola, M. 30, 32
Vartanov, R. V. 26, 33

Wabush 83
Waldram, J. B. 71, 79

Wallerstein, Immanuel 20, 21, 24, 95, 105
Western Europe 44
White Sea 55
Williams, C. H. 70, 79
World Bank 61
world economy 6, 7, 12, 18, 94, 95, 105

world empire 6
world system 2-9, 14, 23, 82, 105
World War II 7, 25

Yakutia 29
Yellowknife 45, 63, 105
Young, Oran R. 32, 39, 48, 75
Yukon 97